PINK FLOYD

BRICKS IN THE WALL

Karl Dallas

BOOKS
A Division Of Shapolsky Publishers

Pink Floyd
Bricks In The Wall

S.P.I. BOOKS
A division of Shapolsky Publishers, Inc.

Previously published by Baton Press, London

ISBN 1-56171-132-2

For any additional information, contact:

S.P.I. BOOKS/Shapolsky Publishers, Inc.
136 West 22nd Street
New York, NY 10011
212/633-2022 / FAX 212/633-2123

Manufactured in Canada

10 9 8 7 6 5 4 3 2 1

CONTENTS

ACKNOWLEDGEMENTS

The author would like to thank the following people for their general help: members of Pink Floyd and especially Roger and Dave, EMI Press Office, Gerald Scarfe, Alan Parker, Miles, Chris Charlesworth, Roy Burchill of Melody Maker, Robert Ellis, Barry Plummer, David Redfern, Jane at Enka, Andy Mabbett of The Amazing Pudding Pink Floyd fanzine (enquiries to 67 Cramlington Road, Great Barr, Birmingham B42 2EE, England, telephone 021-357 9828), and the guy from the record stall in Camden Lock who gave (not sold) me a copy of the Embryo bootleg tape. Needless to say, none of these people necessarily share the author's opinions or conclusions which are entirely his own responsibility.

PART ONE
The Foundations

BRICK I
The End of a Wall

. . . *it's not easy*
Banging your heart against some mad bugger's
Wall.

– Roger Waters

Pink Floyd are finished.

Everyone knows that.

It's not official, of course, even though Roger Waters answers 'I should think so' about whether 'The Final Cut' was really final (he did, after all, deny it, when the album first came out in 1983). The only trouble is that people will keep buying their albums.

It must annoy the music media that the Floyd violate all the principles governing today's music media except one: they are possibly the most prosperous rock and roll band in the world.

Look at the figures, the 'units of product shipped and sold', in the jargon of the biz: over 55 million albums sold in all; 14 million of them 'Dark Side of the Moon', still in the top 200 sellers (and the Guinness Book of Records) 11 years after its release; 13 million copies of the double album, 'The Wall' sold in an even shorter time; and over a million of the so-called failure, 'The Final Cut'. Some of today's one-hit wonders should have such a 'failure'!

They did it, not by bowing to the demand for mindless imitations of the great sounds of black music in yesterday's Detroit or today's Burundi, not by spinning androgynous webs about themselves, not by gobbing actually or metaphorically at their public, not by holding back the years with the electronic equivalent of dowager's facelifts, not by hanging out in the right joints and with the right crowd, not by boozing themselves legless or spiking their arms with snow-white death, but by creating music that taps a nerve and provokes a response, whether you are a deprived kid singing 'We don't need no education', or a survivor from the Falklands.

Pink Floyd have been a flop, in media terms, ever since Syd Barrett left to become a vegetable in Cambridge and they lost their only member to live up to the image of what a rock star should be. It's no wonder they won't give interviews, for what could they say? They live in their big houses and drive their Porsche and Merc cars and send their kids to the right schools, they take their holidays in the same Greek island and they know nothing of the real world.

Yet while the dinosaurs slide into the sand; retiring with dignity (apart from the occasional, much-hyped reunion), the Floyd have kept going, against all predictions, against all logic, moving units of product and putting bums on seats.

Deep Purple is no more, Led Zeppelin has collapsed like a punctured balloon, the Beatles quit while they were still decently ahead, leaving us – what? – the Stones, prancing their geriatric way, Rod Stewart, no longer Rod the Mod but still preening his coxcomb and pretending to be one of the boys, and the Floyd, emerging once every couple of years from somewhere in the Home Countries with another epic of private angst, and reaching a whole new audience with it.

Take any more or less random group of human beings, throw them together because they have one – just one – thing in common, force them to make their careers together because of that, and you have created a potential for mutual hatred that can be observed wherever people have to work together or live together, whether it be a nuclear family or an automobile production line.

Add to that the grinding pressure of life on the road, the lack of sleep, the bad food, the adrenalin flash as the air-conditioned slum of the dressing room is left for the stage, the post-coital depression that follows even the best gigs . . . and how few and far between are those that live up to the expectations of that first, confident step upon the stage! Add to that the emotional pressures of those thousands of souls feeding on your energy, the early call next day, and the rolling landscapes past the limo window: only to be fated with the weary treadmill again. And then the between-tours times: there is the vague but growing anxiety of the clause in the contract stipulating so many albums per year, the necessity to find something *new* to say and the despair when it refuses to come, and the effort to create collectively, in the most alienating, divisive, soul-destroying industry outside of porn-dealing!

When the album finally is done, there is the promotional planning. How can this tour top the last? The photo sessions, the choosing of the single, the interviews with the gentlemen and ladies of the press!

They call themselves critics, but rarely would they measure up to the standards set by Matthew Arnold: (the critics should make a) 'disinterested endeavour to learn and propagate the best that is known and thought in the world' or T. S. Eliot (he will) 'endeavour to discipline his personal prejudices . . . in the common pursuit of true judgement'. Thomas Hood's howl of rage is more appropriate:

What is the modern poet's fate?
To write his thoughts upon a slate;
The critic spits on what is done,
Gives it a wipe – and all is gone.

Why do they do it, these self-styled critics, when so much that they write betrays dislike for a task that their readers would give their eye teeth for?

The rock critic, however (and I speak as one, myself), is more parasite than fighting fish, not only in the unashamed courting of hand-outs, (front-row seats and hotel rooms on tours, T shirts, albums, videos, access to the famous and a little reflected glory on the block,) but also in that he brings nothing to the creative process without which he would have nothing to write about. At worst, they can turn groups against each other, create rivalries where none exist, or just get in the way.

It's natural to see the creative artist's revulsion of the critic as a response to bad reviews: when you have spent a year's toil and thousands of pounds on doing your best, it must be galling to have it rubbished in five lines by some idiot. Good reviews, however, can be as hard to take too, when so often they betray as much insensitivity as bad ones.

I think of Mike Oldfield, the young manic-depressive whose music, created to see him through the bad patches, became a megamillion seller. He told me after his first major interview: 'I feel as if I've been raped.' I think of Tangerine Dream, electronic romantics of the German economic miracle, ringing me up to thank me for a bad review, because 'it's nice to know someone out there was listening'.

I think too of those who have been destroyed by success, some of them really close friends: Sandy Denny . . . Janis Joplin . . . Jim Croce . . . Jimi Hendrix . . . Jim Morrison . . . Tim Hardin . . . Graham Bond . . . Tim Buckley . . . Phil Ochs . . . Bob Marley.

I set their names against those of the great survivors: Bob Dylan . . . Melanie . . . Paul Simon . . . Carl Perkins . . . John McLaughlin . . . Joe Cocker . . . Al Stewart . . . Jack Bruce . . . Arlo Guthrie . . . John Sebastian . . . Mick Jagger . . . Roger Waters . . . Dave Gilmour . . . Kevin Coyne . . . Mike Oldfield.

I must confess I never thought Dylan would make it.

Phil Ochs used to say to me during Dylan's retirement from live performance in the mid-Sixties that Bob would die if he came back to public performance, and it was he himself who persuaded the recluse out of his shell to perform for Chile in 1974. It was Ochs who died two years later, while Dylan lived long enough to be saved, and be born again.

11

In 1965, Ochs wrote: 'One year from now I think it will be very dangerous to Dylan's life to get on the stage. In other words, he's gotten inside so many people's heads – Dylan has become part of so many people's psyche, and there're so many screwed-up people in America, and death is such a part of the American scene now . . .

'It's a form of hypnosis. It's not that everybody sits there listening to him with a single-track mind. Dylan has managed to convene a very dangerous neurotic audience together in one place, who are all hipped to him on different levels. They aren't all listening to him in the same way.

'Some of them are there looking for the lost symbol of the message singer. And none of them really understand: none of them have any right to Dylan. Dylan is an individual singing. And these people want to own him . . .

'It's evil. It's a very sick thing going on there. And it's because of this very neurotic audience that Dylan has got. And that is why Dylan has got to be careful, and that is why he'll have to quit singing.'

It's frightening to me that, in a book published five years before Och's death and nine years before the prediction came true, I warned that if John Lennon stopped keeping a low profile he would surely be assasinated. He did become more public, and on December 8 1980, he *did* die.

One of 19th Century literature's more unhelpful bequests to 20th Century culture is the Byronic image of artist as hero/victim: it gives us a ready made attitude to Tom Chatterton, the marvellous boy, dying of syphilis in his garret, Shelley drowning on the beach at Spezzia, Byron himself dying for Greek liberty at Missolonghi, Rupert Brooke's death (though not from war wounds) at Scyros in 1915 and Dylan's namesake, Thomas, drinking and smoking himself to death on an American lecture tour in 1953, the year that saw the beginnings of rock and roll.

The media are offended by Pink Floyd's refusal to play this game, and words like 'paranoia' spring to their typing fingers. Well, if you are being persecuted, it's not always paranoid to be aware of the fact. And if Roger Waters tries to stop people taking his photograph because he wants to walk down the road without being recognised, if he wants his children at school spared the notoriety of having a rock and roll millionaire for a father, if he wants to add nothing to the fictionalised references to his own emotional traumas in 'The Wall' and 'The Pro's and Cons of Hitch Hiking', then he's doing what many have sought to do before him: to let his work stand as its own defence, and to keep his private life private. He and his peers have, after all, had enough bad experiences with the music press to excuse a little paranoia. When I was in Germany with the Floyd in 1977 on the 'Animals' tour, everyone was a barrel of laughs but Roger. We had dinner together, the visiting guests of EMI, the management, and three of the band, but he didn't come. I wondered why he was being so distant, especially since I'd just given the new album an enthusiastic review. It turned out that he hadn't read it.

But a few days after my return, I received the following missive, written on Lufthansa airmail paper, clearly on the plane home:

'Dear Karl Dallas

This is the first and probably the last time I shall write to a member of your normally ignoble calling. I thought your piece on 'Animals' in the MM was extremely perceptive, lucid and humane. To at last receive such tangible evidence that someone has copped it all, and explained it all so well to the great unwashed, lightened the load no end:

Thank you!

Yours sincerely,
Roger Waters'

The rest of the paper was given over to a sketch from inside the plane of a sunrise through the window, a bearded character in a woolly hat with the letters 'MM' on it (me, presumably), on the outside looking in.

A fan letter, yet.

As he has explained to me many times, there is no need for them to play the media game. They achieved those record sales figures without exposing themselves to the gruelling, time-wasting routine of interviews by rote, in which the record company hires a suite in a major hotel and rows the hacks in, one after another, to ask the same old questions: the coming tour . . . the last album . . . how they are getting on with each other . . . don't they think they're past it and shouldn't they retire while they're still ahead?

This, to borrow the quotation from 'Julius Caesar' which inspired the title of their last album, is the unkindest cut of all. We (and I speak for all my fellow hacks) tolerate the inspired mindgames Dylan plays with us, because the more he juggles his light bulb and answers the simplest question like a gnomic oracle, he is in a perverse way acknowledging our importance, however difficult and inaccessible he purports to be.

What we find hard to take from the Floyd is their yawning unconcern with what we think, because even our kindest words will have small impact on sales. Of the millions who buy a Floyd album, how many have bothered to read a review? Ten thousand? A hundred thousand at most? And, let's face it, how many of the press have been aware enough of the sharp end of rock to earn the right to have their comments taken seriously on any development in its checkered and lurching history?

13

(There is a sad tradition that dates back to the days when the rock press was concerned mostly with jazz: Leonard Feather's dismissal of the significance of John Coltrane's innovations is the example that springs most readily to mind, but there are many more.) Reggae was dismissed at editorial conferences as mindless and boring music for skinheads (as if that made any difference to what came out of the grooves!) and punk likewise. And though much play is now made of the 'golden age' of Floyd down at UFO as a stick to beat their later, more successful productions, you'll search in vain through the files of the music press in the Sixties (apart from the underground media, like IT, who went overboard in the opposite direction and indulged *their* bands' every whim to show that they were aware of what was going on.

To my recollection, only one man, Nick, the young son of veteran jazz critic Max Jones, recognised what was happening, and he in such over-heated prose that most of his effusions could be printed only in America's Rolling Stone. It's significant, perhaps, that he was frozen out of the UK press, and today he works as a record company publicist — one of the best, by the way.

There is a whole genre of rock music, heavy metal, which is given scant attention by most of the press, apart from the occasional token article. In many ways, however, heavy metal is today's true underground. Only look at the grassroots strength it has among the fans, and at the universal disparagement it receives at the hands of the media. And yet, for all its faults, metal is a music in the mainstream of rock's development which can be traced back to the blues bands of Cream, Graham Bond, and Cyril Davies. Anyone with any sense of rock's traditions would have to acknowledge its significance, if only as a sociological phenomenon: a music that maintains itself within its own defined constituency, regardless of how much or how little media attention it receives. It is not unique in this: folk, jazz and country inhabit similar ghettos, though hardly of comparable size.

To a certain extent, Floyd have their own ghetto, larger than all of these, and it is closer to heavy metal than to anything else (hardly surprising, since Dave Gilmour is probably the world's finest heavy metal guitarist). On the backs of the leather jacket worn by its largely working-class, male audience you will see the names of metal bands like Styx and Motorhead, even on the Waters solo tour. (There are also plenty of Gilmour T-shirts: Floyd fans find it quite easy, apparently, to share their loyalties between their two estranged heroes.)

The noisy enthusiasm which greets their music is like that at the loudest metal concert; strange when one considers that the monumental nature of the Floyd/Waters presentation diminishes the visible stature of the performers on stage and makes guitar hero posing impossible.

Perhaps it is the essentially working-class nature of their following that alienates the media, whose writers are would-be Yuppies – Young Upwardly Mobile Professionals. They will pay lip service to the wilder extremes of the political left in a middle class, strictly unproletarian way, yet one knows that their revolutionism is an infantile delusion that would be blown away by the sombre realities of actual social change. This is why a real working-class phenomenon frightens them, literally. Pink Floyd, and especially its lyricist Roger Waters, had a message that went to the heart of the young working class.

Having started from the most effete and airy-fairy beginnings in art school hops and lightshow and drugs dominated clubs in the affluent Sixties, instead of vanishing up the same orifice that swallowed so many of their peers, they developed a high-tech method of communication which spoke directly to the same generation that were to swell the ranks of Margaret Thatcher's dole queues in the more bitter times ahead.

Undoubtedly, there was an element of bread and circuses in their spectacles, for if you can save ten quid from your GIRO cheque and let the loud, quadraphonic music envelop you, and the powerfully animated visuals suck you into their reality, it makes it easier to cope with the increasingly aggressive policing, inner-city decay, unemployment and imminent nuclear destruction outside the concert hall. The world of Floyd, moreover, is one that holds that outside 'reality' up to hatred, ridicule and contempt: see the world statesmen girating in slow motion to the tune of 'The lunatic is on the grass', the marching hammers of Gerald Scarfe's frightening vision of 'The Wall', or the metal dinosaur scrabbling across a lunar landscape for 'Welcome to the Machine'.

'It's only a fucking rock and roll band,' exclaimed Roger Waters, refusing to mourn its passing.

Don't you believe it!

BRICK II
Lose Your Mind and Play

I know it's only rock and roll, but I like it.
— the Rolling Stones

The proposition that 'rock and roll will stand' (Jon Landau), may be justifiable in the sense that 'classics' like 'Great Balls of Fire' and 'Johnny B. Goode' can still evoke a knee-jerk response from certain types of audience (thus preventing Jerry Lee Lewis and Chuck Berry from being as seminal influences in this thirtieth year of rock as they were in its beginnings), but as Landau himself has pointed out, the attempt to see rock as high art has led it seriously astray. Lennon and McCartney may have been the greatest songwriters since Schubert, as Tony Palmer claims, but since they were writing in a different tradition, does the comparison *mean* anything?

In one sense, of course, such comparisons *can* be valid, because whatever their lasting contribution to the development of music many of the classical 'greats' were, in a very real sense, pop stars. It is the later generations who have enshrouded their memory in such deep reverence that any sense of fun is lost. No wonder they call it 'serious' music.

The near-riot that greeted the première of Stravinsky's 'Rite of Spring' is evidence of the way pre-rock music engaged loyalties in a way that is inconceivable today, even though concert attendances are higher now than then. No one would riot, today, at the première of a new work by Stockhausen, say, or Philip Glass. The cultists go to wonder; the unconvinced stay away. Even Frank Zappa conducting the London Philharmonic Orchestra raises scarcely an eyebrow, despite the scatological nature of much of his work. (He did get banned from the Royal Albert Hall, but that's mainly because on a previous trip one of the band had broken open the Great Organ and desecrated it by playing 'Louie Louie' on it).

The music that people do get worked up about today is rock and roll, though I doubt if they will ever again make themselves look as silly as they did over the Sex Pistols. The numbers of people involved are huge, of course, compared with the attendance at classical events, but then, as I've said, so are attendances at Tchaikovsky concerts, compared with anything that extends the frontiers of music as Pyotr Ilyich did in his day. Indeed, once someone has got into the megabucks bracket, like Dylan or the Floyd, they tend to be left alone, and it's the little people, the fringe theatre and black dance groups, who attract the attention of the contemporary book-burners.

One explanation for why the megastars have virtually total license is that their work is counter-revolutionary in effect, whatever it may appear to be saying. As the dynamic duo of revolutionary criticism, Julie Birchill and Tony Parsons, wrote in their self-styled obituary of rock and roll for the Trotskyist Pluto Press: 'In "rock and roll", the particular interests of the establishment and capitalism fit together as compactly as a joint, finding an affinity that they are unable to achieve in any other business venture . . . By maintaining the music's illusion of youth rebellion it accomplishes its purpose – a green-back producer channelling not only the money but the time, energy and psyche of young people into what has been their most jealously guarded palliative for over 20 years.' ('The Boy Looked at Johnny', 1978)

This estimate of commercial popular music is defensible only if one ignores the context in which it is performed. Popular art can often be more illuminating of its time than any high art. I quote an example from history:

Most people know the old music hall song, 'My Old Dutch', with its saccharine reference to marital bliss:

> *We've been together now for forty years,*
> *And it don't seem a day too much –*
> *An' there ain't a lady living in the land*
> *As I'd swap for my dear old Dutch!*

It was written and sung by Albert Chevalier, the great music hall 'Coster's Laureate' who died in 1923, and Colin McInnes, an admirer, could not ignore the 'lugubrious' tune and the 'oleaginous dollops of sentiment' with which it was delivered. But, as McInnes points out, the real significance of the song, lost on those who would see us return to similar traditional values lies in its preamble.

'To a soft whine of violins under-playing the central theme, the tabs part and you see a drop inscribed WORKHOUSE. In this there are cut two doors, one marked MEN, the other WOMEN. Sitting before the drop is the workhouse porter (appearing at thirty shillings a week, since his isn't a speaking part) when, lo and behold, in totter Albert and his Dutch (she probably at twenty shillings a week, since she doesn't speak

17

either), and Albert presents his admittance cards to the porter. This functionary glances severely at the old pair (a tremolo from the French horn now joining the violins), and indicates with a rough gesture that they must now enter the workhouse doors.

'BUT, Albert has not noticed that there are *two* entrances: and tries to go with his ancient spouse to the one marked MEN. Whereupon the porter tries to separate them roughly, and push the aged Dutch into the door marked WOMEN. The full horror of the situation dawns on Albert, who cries: 'You can't do this to *us* – we've been together FOR FORTY YEARS'. A curtain now cuts off the porter and the donah (who nip round to the pub for a half quartern), and Albert advances to the footlights, despair yet determination on his honest features and, as the orchestra moves into its big moment, thus begins . . .' ('Sweet Saturday Night', MacGibbon & Kee, 1967)

More people must have heard Chevalier's song, and thereby his commentary upon the iniquities of the Poor Law system than read Engels' 'Condition of the Working Class in England'. Whether hearing the song played much of a part in reforming the system, however, is open to argument.

Although the urban music hall tradition is still poorly documented and hence poorly understood, we do have the evidences of sheet music and other contemporary writings to draw on. But thanks to the nature of the electronic medium, we have almost instant access to any single moment in the past three decades of rock and roll, so that the barrier between past and present becomes blurred. Popular culture is no longer ephemeral.

In its negative sense, of course, this is the reason for the cult of nostalgia: commercial culture's biggest growth industry. If you want to live in the past, you can relive the big band era, the skiffle era, rockabilly of Sun records in Memphis, Tennessee, the Fifties, the Sixties, the Seventies, the Eighties, the Nineties . . .

Hang on! We haven't got there yet!

The image of the past presented by nostalgic recreations is often not just a travesty of the truth, unrecognisable to anyone who was there at the time, but contains fallacies in its presentation which prevent us from properly understanding our own present. Look at the way the phrase 'Victorian values' has been made to represent a return to some kind of moral standards, when the truth of the Victorian era can be found in the child mortality (and child prostitution) statistics, the lack of law and order for those who couldn't afford to buy it, the gerrymandering of elections, the persecution of trades unionists, and the exploitation of what is now called the Third World, with consequences we are still paying for today.

18

Culture is more than a key to understanding the past. It tells us something significant about ourselves.

Pop of the pre-rock era did this but rarely, which is why it is often derided as 'moon and June' music because of the sloppy sentimentality and clichés of its rhyming schemes. But realistic songs like 'My Old Dutch' are not unique. 'Brother Can You Spare a Dime?', 'Ten Cents a Dance', 'Strange Fruit', and 'The House I Live In' are occasional glimpses of reality through the windows of the Brill Building or a Tin Pan Alley basement. Indeed, the entire history of British pop publishing begins when Lawrence Wright paid a street singer a few quid for a lugubrious street ballad, 'Don't Go Down the Mine Daddy', about a mining disaster.

Rock and Roll, however, made the socially significant lyric the rule rather than the exception, so that one of the differences between pop and rock is that rock songs are *about* something, while pop songs aren't about anything much. (And if the sceptic doubts this, noticing that most rock songs, too, are about sexual encounters of one kind or another, I'd have to agree. A song like 'Work With Me Annie', though, among many others, which describes almost explicitly a couple's mutual search for satisfaction is actually in the advance guard of the sexual revolution, as against any commercial lovesong of the previous decade. Not only the lyrics take on this role; the instruments do too. The tremolo-bar jangle of Mick Green's guitar on Johnny Kidd's 'Shakin' All Over' spoke directly to the loins of an entire generation of early rockers.)

If Marshall McLuhan is to be believed (and though he's unfashionable today, he said more sensible things about the electronic era than any of his detractors, or imitators, will admit), rock was a revolutionary form, not so much because of its content, but because the very nature of the electronic medium involved the audience in a way that hadn't been seen since the days of the great folk bards.

Both the old epic and the 12-bar riff had this in common: they were basically oral media, with the written word (Homer's noting down of the old Hellenic tales, or song lyrics on an album sleeve) merely the handmaiden of the real, living thing.

McLuhan also explained that the growth of stereo hifi contributed to this new seriousness in content: 'When a medium becomes a means of depth experience the old categories of "classical" and "popular" or of "highbrow" and "lowbrow" no longer obtain,' he wrote in 1962. 'When LP and hifi and stereo arrived, a depth approach also came in . . .'

('Understanding Media')

People talk about the Beatles, but undoubtedly the single performer who led the way to commercial acceptance of more serious subject matter was Bob Dylan. As Josh Dunson said after Dylan's first album had sold 150,000 copies, and Peter Paul and Mary's recording of 'Blowin' in the Wind' sold a million, 'His success forced other large commercial companies to listen to the audition tapes of topical singers with more interest than they had previously shown. Dylan had forced his songs and his contemporaries into the mass media.' ('Freedom in the Air', International Publishers, N. Y., 1965) After coming into contact with Dylan during their first US trip, Lennon and McCartney composed the Dylan-inspired 'I'm Down'.

The other thing that distinguished rock was that 'audiences or creators can determine the content of a popular art communicated through the mass media,' as Charlie Gillett wrote in 'The Sound of the City', the most important – probably the only important – book about rock. 'The businessmen who mediate between the audience and the creator can be forced by either to accept a new style. The rise of rock and roll is proof.' And so, though the music business was slow to come to terms with what was happening . . . for a long time Bob Dylan, discovered by John Hammond, was dubbed 'Hammond's folly' within the big grey CBS building in New York, until the sales figures came in, that is – eventually they decided that they could make a buck out of this kind of thing as readily as any other. And so the rock poets became incorporated into the market system. They had no beef: it gave them huge audiences, larger than any other poet had ever had before, even Dylan Thomas in his heyday. Interestingly, the only previous comparison would be Vladimir Mayakovsky in the Soviet Union in the 1920s.

You can't blame the artists for grabbing their opportunities with both hands: anyone who thinks people like starving in garrets for their art just hasn't met any artists. And apart from the odd dilettante, the artist wants to reach an audience. Money is not so much the issue here as feedback, the response, in laughter or tears or jeers, which indicates that some kind of contact has been established. The real irony of mass circulation rock is that it provides money in plenty, but feedback becomes less and less possible as fame and fortune increase.

Pink Floyd were victims of this basic contradiction in the mass marketing of art. At the time of the recording of 'Saucerful of Secrets', EMI staff producer Norman Smith was going round talking about forcing them to 'knuckle down and get something together' after the self-indulgences of this second album.

As Roger Waters tells it: 'It was the actual title track of 'A Saucerful of Secrets' which gave us our second breath. We had finished the whole album. The company wanted the whole thing to be a follow-up to the first. But what we wanted to do was this longer piece. And it was given to us by the company like sweeties after we'd finished; we could do what we liked with the last 12 minutes.

'It was the first thing we'd done without Syd (Barrett) that we thought was any good.'

In fact, it's pretty inconsequential and consists mainly of almost random assemblings of keyboard work by Rick Wright (as he said, 'we go into the studio with absolutely nothing and we sit around saying Look, we're gonna write something, with no preconceived ideas'), processed electronically, with some wordless voices at the end, though it certainly led the way to the mastery of 'Echoes' on 'Meddle', three years later.

Despite the reputation 'Saucer' gave them as musical revolutionaries, they have never been innovative, as I wrote of them at the time of the 1977 'Animals' tour, '. . . but then they never claimed to be. Their use of electronics adds very little to the musical vocabulary. Their melodies are tonal, their harmonies consonant; their rhythms (with the notable exception of 'Money') four-square and almost flat-footed.

'And yet, somehow, using all these well-tried devices, they nevertheless indicate widening horizons.

'On the other hand, they are not really the greatest live band in the world, well though they play. If it were not for the necessity to go on the road promoting their albums, they could actually confine their work to the studio without any great loss to anyone. They make few obvious attempts to communicate, a failure which the proliferation of visual effects is presumably meant to fill.

'The improved sound, if anything, heightens the sense of being at home listening to the album if you close your eyes for an instant, and while the solos are longer, the greater freedom doesn't necessarily produce anything of greater moment than in the narrower compass of the album.

'And yet, here again, their very ordinariness on stage puts their work back into a human perspective. If they were the proverbial superhuman titans bestriding the auditorium like colossi, they would be unbearable.' Of course, that's what many of the audience wanted, which is why a Canadian boy on that very tour found himself being spat on in the face by an enraged Roger Waters.

Though they didn't originate the concept album – that dubious honour belongs, arguably, to the Pretty Things' 'S. F. Sorrow', which inspired Pete Townshend to write his 'rock opera' (oratorio, strictly speaking), 'Tommy' – during this period they were edging towards longer structures covering an entire LP side, like 'Atom Heart Mother' in 1970, 'Echoes' on 'Meddle' (1971), and then a whole album, 'Dark Side of the Moon' (1973).

Undoubtedly, the trend has been influenced by their work for films. At the time of the release of the 'Obscured By Clouds' soundtrack in '72, Dave Gilmour told an interviewer: 'We've had huge arguments about what exactly to do on some of those soundtrack albums and other albums. Some of us thought we should put songs on them, others thought we should turn the whole thing into a one-subject concept for the whole album. That's the way they worked out.

'Roger has certainly got a bit of an obsession about making the whole album into a one-subject deal, into what you might call a concept album.' It was over this time, too, that Roger Waters began to have something significant to say: about the difficulties of personal relationships, about deaths during the war, about the facelessness of modern education, about madness. Put like that, the subject matter sound boringly like the sort of introspective navel-gazing that had disfigured a lot of singer songwriters, but Waters was a bit old for that kind of juvenilia. And unlike the solo songwriter, Waters was able to command enormous forces to underpin what he had to say: not merely three excellent fellow musicians in the band, Gilmour especially being one of the finest, but also an increasingly complex stage show, embracing quadraphonic sound, lights, back-projected live action and specially animated film, gigantic blow-up figures and the like.

What came across, more and more, however, was the alienation. The positive side of what he had to say achieved less attention. And the increasing hugeness of the halls they were playing not only alienated the band from their audience. It alienated them from each other, too.

Water turned this very alienation into 'The Wall', a major work which became a top-selling double album, a vast stage show in which an actual wall of cardboard bricks was built between the band and the audience, and a powerful movie, also available on video, in which Bob Geldof played 'Pink', a rock 'n' roll musician. The name comes from a joke about an early candidate for management who asked them, apparently, 'Which one is Pink?' The phrase occurs in an earlier song, 'Have a Cigar', from 'Wish You Were Here'.

To dramatise the fact that in such large venues the audience had hardly any idea of whom they were listening to, Waters had much of the music played by a 'surrogate band' of session musicians, and he was right, few in the halls knew the difference.

'Actually, the idea was that they were meant to be what we became,' he told me in 1982. 'At that junction Pink was like a gestalt figure, and that was really a kind of theatrical shock tactic at the beginning of the show, because people would assume that it was us and ask: 'Why are they dressed in those weird clothes? What's going on?' And wonder about things. 'I just wanted to create a sort of confused atmosphere at the beginning so that people could start to sort it out slowly as the show went on. What I liked about doing 'The Wall' and why it was different from touring in '77 which we did with 'Animals' and 'Wish You Were Here', which were also fairly rigidly constructed pieces, was that in 'The Wall' we provided the audience with enough stuff so that it was almost impossible not to be involved in it.

'And that was what the intention was, really, to do a rock show which didn't have to rely necessarily on the feeling of being in the presence of divine beings, or getting some contact-high from being close to power and wealth and fame . . .'

So, in the end, the history of Pink Floyd matters because they tried to buck the power structure, using the greatest resources that the power structure has ever offered, then or since. And they failed.

They succeeded in getting the people to come to their concerts, to buy millions of albums which have something very significant to say about what it is like to live in a modern industralised society.

I suspect they failed to get people to *listen* to what they had to say, as opposed to how they said it, the content rather than the form, because what they wanted to say was something you end up having to say outside and against the structures they were using. An understanding of why that is so is also an understanding of the world we live in, and of how to change it to one where different structures will be available for artists to communicate their vision.

BRICK III
The Dream Is Over

> *. . . I have to admit*
> *I was just a little afraid, oh yeah*
> *But then . . .*
> – The Pro's and Cons of Hitch-hiking

Let me tell you the way it was in the Sixties, because most people get it wrong.

For most people it was a revolution that failed. But in reality, from where I sat, it was a counter-revolution that finally succeeded in killing what Roger Waters was to describe, in 'The Final Cut', as the postwar dream.

The real revolution took place during the final years of the war, even as Eric Fletcher Waters, Roger's soldier father, was dying on the beach at Anzio, and Roger was being born, in 1944. That was the year of R. A. Butler's Education Act, implemented by the postwar Labour Government in 1947, which sent the brightest and best of the previously deprived into the nation's grammar schools – to come streaming out again as early members of the rock generation. They were kids who'd been taught to lay hands on the mechanism of society, and they thought it was time to take delivery of the promise.

But already, as GIs and Ivans celebrated on the Elbe, as Clem Attlee's Labour Government was taking power with its seemingly unassailable majority of 168 and 13¼ million votes in 1945, and as Nye Bevan was bringing in the National Health Service in 1948, the irreversible social revolution was proving to be all too temporary: Winston Churchill was back in charge by October '51, the alliances of victory were being dismantled in the cold peace, the resistance movements of Europe and Asia were disarmed, the first American bombers targetted east of Germany landed in Norfolk, the first American troops landed in South Korea.

Six weeks before Bill Haley recorded 'Rock Around the Clock' in New York's Pythian Temple on April 12 1954 – initially a flop, until it was used in the movie, 'The Blackboard Jungle', after which it sold 17 million copies – America exploded the H-bomb at Bikini atoll. The day after Lonnie Donegan's 'My Old Man's a Dustman' hit number one in the UK charts, South African police shot and killed seventy black demonstrators in Sharpeville, and wounded 150 more. That was in March 1960.

Actually, that first year of the Sixties doesn't read like much of a rollcall of social progress. It's true, a number of African nations achieved some kind of independence (though not from the multinationals), and Harold Macmillan tried to tell the South African Parliament about the wind of change those geographical and political facts represented. The Labour Party conference voted for disarmament. John Kennedy was elected US President.

But see what else happened:

January:	French army mutiny in Algeria.
February:	French atomic test in the Sahara. US ballistic missile early warning system set up on Fylingdales Moor.
March:	Sharpeville.
May:	US spy plane shot down over USSR. US underground nuclear tests resumed. Breakdown of Paris summit. Army coup in Turkey.
June:	Britain launches first guided missile-equipped destroyer. Parliament rejects Wolfenden recommendations to decriminalise homosexuality.
July:	Army mutiny in Congo.
August:	Military coup in Laos.
September:	Congolese president Lumumba dismissed.
October:	Royal Navy's first nuclear submarine launched.
November:	Agreement on stationing of US Polaris missile submarines at Holy Loch on the Clyde.
December:	Lumumba kidnapped and (in February 1961) murdered on CIA orders.

The Beatles had signed with Brian Epstein, but they hadn't been allowed to play at the Cavern yet. The Everley Brothers' 'Cathy's Clown' was a UK number one in April. America's first disco, the Whisky-a-Go-Go, opened on Sunset Boulevard in Los Angeles January, complete with mini-skirted go-go girls in cages. 'Teen Angel' by Mark Denning (who?) was a US no. 1. Frank Sinatra welcomed Elvis out of the army with a TV special, 'Welcome Home, Elvis'. Rock pioneer DJ Alan Freed was accused of accepting payola. Hank Ballard and the Moonlighters, who'd given white singers like Georgia Gibbs a model of black sexuality to rip off and sanitise in their 'Work With Me, Annie' in 1954 (they also invented the Twist), achieved a short-lived record by having three singles in Billboard's Hot Hundred chart at the same time. Later, the Beatles got the top five places, of course. The

25

Miracles got Tamla Motown its first million seller with 'Shop Around'. The Drifters' 'Save the Last Dance For Me' was a US no. 1. So was the Shirelles' version of Carole King's 'Will You Still Love Me Tomorrow?'. It was a year before Bob Dylan was to make his first recording at a friend's home.

A few good tunes, you'd say, but a pretty average year.

In 1960, Roger Waters was 16, Nick Mason and Rick Wright were 15, Syd Barrett was 14 and so was Dave Gilmour, to come into the story later. Syd and Dave met at about that time, though they were at different schools. Roger was at the same school as Dave, but they didn't know each other then, as Roger was two years older. This was in spite of the fact that Syd and Dave and Roger had all gone to the same Saturday morning art class for a year or two.

Like many of those who were to emerge as spokespersons for the products of the new Education Act – Mick Jagger of the London School of Economics was another – Barrett, Gilmour and Waters were hardly typical of their generation, and nor were Wright or Mason.

Rick Wright went to Haberdashers before Regent Street Polytechnic, where he met Waters and Mason. Nick Mason went to Frensham Heights and owned an Aston Martin and a Lotus Elan by the time Floyd were starting. Waters' mother was a teacher and so was Gilmour's mother, before she became a film editor. Dave's father was a professor of genetics.

We may think we know something of Waters' mother because of what he has shown us in 'The Wall', but he's somewhat apologetic about that portrayal, which he says was not drawn directly from his own experience.

It's interesting that Syd Barrett, as well as Dave Gilmour, who was to replace him, were the members who displayed most devotion to rock music in their earlier days. Rick Wright had just two weeks' piano tuition and Roger Waters went for two Spanish guitar lessons at the Spanish Guitar Centre in London, 'but I couldn't do with all that practice'. The first tune he remembers learning to play was 'Shanty Town'. Nick Mason studied piano and flute as a child.

Syd's parents bought him a banjo when he was 11, and when Dave was 13 he acquired a cheap Spanish guitar from a next-door neighbour. He'd already become a rock fan: 'I got hit over the head by rock and roll music when I was ten. 'Rock Around the Clock', I think, was the first one that made a marked difference to my life, which I had on a 78. The au pair girl sat on it and broke it, for which she was never forgiven.'

Dave and Syd had known each other since they were 14 and started playing together regularly when Syd got into the art department of the local technical college while Dave was trying (unsuccessfully, as it turned out) to pass his A-levels in a different part of the same building.

'We were there together for two years, and we spent all our lunchtimes playing together, learning the latest riffs,' Dave recalls.

Later, when he replaced Syd, Dave was on the receiving end of a certain amount of flak from Barrett fans who felt he wasn't as interesting a guitarist as his predecessor. Not surprisingly, of course, he rejects this view: 'I had far better technique than him. I would teach him a lot of things, and that was very early days for him. As he progressed, his technique never progressed nearly as far as his inventiveness did.'

Another time, he complained about 'people saying that I pinched his style when our backgrounds are so similar.

'We spent a lot of time together as teenagers listening to the same music,' he explained at the time. 'Our influences are pretty much the same. I don't want to go into print saying that I taught Syd Barrett everything he knows, 'cause it's patently untrue, but there are one or two things in Syd's style that I know came from me.

'All the people around at that time were just starting to be in bands. There were others who were very much better and very good at it, even in those days.'

Syd made himself an amplifier to go with his new electric guitar when he was 15, and by the next year he was playing with Geoff Mott and the Mottoes, one of those 'legendary Cambridge bands' you hear so much about. He also played bass with another local outfit, the Hollering Blues. Dave's first band was called the Newcomers, with 'hi-fi' speaker corner cabinets with three little legs, from someone's living room with a tiny amp in the back, so it would blow up every two minutes, start humming and buzzing and walk across the stage by itself'. Later he had his own band, Jokers Wild, but at that time Floyd were already coming home to play at May Balls in Cambridge, like veritable conquering heroes. Rick, Nick and Roger had met at Regent Street Polytechnic, where they were all studying architecture. Nick and Rick had a flat together in Highgate, which was later passed on to Roger, and to Syd, at different times.

The three students formed a band with Roger on lead guitar, Rick on rhythm guitar, Nick on drums, plus Clive Metcalf on bass, with Keith Noble and Juliette Gale, who later became Mrs Wright, as singers. First they were known as Sigma 6 ('available for clubs and parties' it said on the visiting cards handed out by their manager – yes, they even had a manager, Ken Chapman, who also wrote their material). Then they were the T-Set, the Meggadeaths (Roger was, after all, a CND supporter from way back), and then the Architectural Abdabs, abbreviated to just the Abdabs. They were primarily intended to be a rhythm'n'blues band.

In an interview for the student mag Roger offered such musical opinions as 'It is easier to express yourself rhythmically in blues-style. It doesn't need practice, just basic understanding. Rock is just beat without expression though admittedly rhythm and blues forms the basis of original rock.'

The Abdabs broke up when Juliette and Nick got married. By that time, Syd was studying art at Camberwell and had moved into the Highgate flat (now tenanted by Roger) with a mate, a Poly student called Bob Close. Bob was a competent guitarist, though his tastes ran towards traditional jazz. A new band was formed and given the name, at the suggestion of Syd, of Pink Floyd.

Possibly following the example of John Lennon's story of a dream about a steaming pie and the cry 'And they shall be called the Silver Beatles with an "a"', Syd liked to spin legends about how they got their name, but it was quite simple, really: the name was taken from two of Syd's bluesmen heroes, Pink Anderson (born 1900, died 1974, most famous tune 'South Forest Boogie') and Floyd 'Dipper Boy' Council (born 1911, died 1976, also known as the Devil's Daddy-in-Law and Blind Boy Fuller's Buddy).

Roger was demoted from lead to rhythm to bass. Bob Close left after a short time, and by the time they played their first gig in late 1965, at the Countdown Club, they were down to just the four of them, Syd, Roger, Rick and Nick. 'We played from eight till one in the morning with a 20-minute break in the middle. We were paid £15 for that.'

By then, Nick Mason had joined the 18 per cent drop-out rate in British higher education, and was concentrating on music. Roger Waters, too, was losing interest in architecture: 'The practice of architecture is such a compromise in this country, with economics winning, that I just got pissed off with it. So then we all started spending all our grants on equipment.'

It's important to understand why the art schools played such a significant role in the growth of rock and roll – why, to quote a Pete Brown song title, 'The art school dance goes on for ever'.

For a start, there was the sheer number of art students, about 120,000 spread across 159 different kinds of colleges, or roughly a quarter of the total number of students in higher education. The art schools crystallised the differences between the old-style higher education and the new. In the swinging, pragmatic world of Harold Wilson's 1964 Labour Government the Conservative Macmillan government had 'collapsed in a turmoil of TV satire, security and sex scandals, and general irreverent rage at the tired old "upper-class Establishment". Harold Wilson's promise of a "classless, dynamic New

Britain", forged out of "the white heat of technology" seemed to offer our own prospect of a bright "New Frontier" future'. (Jeremy Sandford, preface to 'The Seventies')

The effect of this on the art schools was outlined by Tom Nairn, a lecturer at Hornsey (the college which provided some of Floyd's early light shows, incidentally) until he was expelled after the sit-in of summer, 1968, in which he played a prominent part: 'Society's sharp new interest in many forms of design has created a violent new careerism in these design-arts. Youthful fortunes can be made overnight, through the right ideas, the right scene, aggressiveness in the right place.

'The high-pressure professionalism of fashion has replaced the old doddering philosophy of the artisan. This has had immediate repercussions among art students, producing in some quarters a kind of counter-revolution against the old image of the inspired misfit.

'Here, the hard-boiled competitiveness of the neo-capitalist environment outside, its concern with "image" and "public relations", its frank commodity-fetishism and cult of flash success – all tend to be reproduced in startling miniature in today's art college.

'So while some students dream of being Rembrandt, more assume they are going to be Mary Quants, David Baileys, or David Hockneys. The ethos of art colleges is part a fossilized old world, part the bitchy new one of the ad-man, the teen-age glossy, and the newest gimmick.' ('Student Power', Penguin Special, 1969)

Sounds a lot like rock and roll, doesn't it?

By the time Floyd started playing regularly, of course, the Sixties were already half over. Kennedy had been assassinated two years before, Roy Jenkins' 1959 Obscene Publications Act had freed the public, its children, and even its servants (in the words of the prosecutor, Mervyn Griffith-Jones) to read the thirty 'fucks' or 'fuckings', fourteen 'cunts', thirteen 'balls', six 'shits', six 'arses', four 'cocks' and three 'pisses' (Griffith-Jones' calculations, and I'll take his word for it) in D. H. Lawrence's 'Lady Chatterley's Lover', prosecuted and acquitted in 1960.

But the Lord Chamberlain was still conducting the ridiculous task of censoring stage plays as he'd been doing since 1737, insisting on the deletion of two scenes, 12 'Christs', three 'sods' and two 'get stuffeds' from Edward Bond's 'Saved' before it could be put on at the Royal Court in the autumn of 1965. The subterfuge of making it a club performance didn't work; they were prosecuted successfully, but given a conditional discharge with 50 guineas' costs to pay.

'Fanny Hill' had been successfully prosecuted in November '63, with the result that it wasn't available in paperback until it crept back into the catalogue in '70 – though it had been available all along in a hardback edition, presumably too expensively for children and servants. Mr Griffith-Jones would have approved.

It may have seemed like a revolution at the time, but the mixture was strictly Curate's egg. With the benefit of two decades of hindsight, the reforms don't seem so profound; more like the clearing away of the more obvious detritus of 18th and 19th Century attitudes. Space was being left for a more *contemporary* kind of repression than these obviously outmoded Mrs Grundys could mete out; the time of Mary Whitehouse and the Festival of Light would come.

There was, of course, the problem of all those over-educated art school kids, who were demanding more and more change. There were ways of dealing with *them*, however: drugs.

Drugs had been around a long time before they came to be seen as a chemical short-cut to utopia. Cannabis was in use in China 2000 years before the birth of Christ, and John Allegro has even suggested that Jesus himself was actually a psychedelic mushroom. It is said that witches rubbed themselves on the sensitive parts of the body, like the armpits and the walls of the vagina, with an ointment designed to give them the hallucination that they were flying. George Washington cultivated Indian hemp, cannabis sativa, in his garden and Victorian ladies used to drink hemp tea to ease period pains. In the Middle Ages, ergot poisoning, caused by the fungus *claviceps purpure* on bread grains, caused widespread delirium. It was this mould that Dr Albert Hofman was working on in 1938, when he first isolated the active ingredient, dlysergic acid diethylamide, now more usually abbreviated as LSD or acid.

He carried on working on it and on April 16 1943 he accidently ingested some of the substance, and literally 'tripped' on his four-mile cycle ride home.

At the same time, SS experimenters in the Dachau concentration camp were trying out the effects of mescaline, derived from the South American sacred peyotl cactus, 'to eliminate the will of the person examined' and, on May 27 1943 the Office of Strategic Services, ancestors of today's CIA, fed cannabis to a New York gangster, August Del Gracio, in an attempt to find a mind-bending drug that would make its subjects more amenable under interrogation. It worked fine.

In January 1962, an article by Dr E. James Lieberman, a psychiatrist, in the Bulletin of Atomic Science on 'Psycho-Chemicals as Weapons' warned of 'catastrophic damage that would be neither reversible nor humane', calling forth a rebuttal from Dr Timothy Leary, the drugs guru, accusing the author of spreading 'serious confusion in the minds of a credulous public and a credulous military'.

'. . . consciousness-expanding chemicals, far from being dangerous weapons,' he wrote, 'may produce dramatic changes in personality leading to unprecented peace, sanity, and happiness . . .

'If an enemy drops LSD in the water supply and if you are accurately informed and prepared, then you . . . should sit back and enjoy the most exciting educational experience of your life (you might be forever grateful to the saboteur) . . .

'If an enemy introduced a consciousness-expanding drug into a military command centre, our leaders – if they are accurately informed and experienced about the potentials of expanded awareness – might find that men in certain key positions could function better . . .'

Unfortunately for Dr Leary's credibility (such as it is, today), information since released in America under the Freedom of Information Act has revealed not only that research funded by the CIA and the US armed forces was responsible for several deaths and countless (because not counted by the authorities) disturbed lives, but that it was this research that led to the widespread experimentation with hallucinogenics among potential revolutionaries throughout the western world.

On April 13, 1953 Allen Dulles, director of the CIA, approved the MKULTRA programme for the 'covert use of biological and chemical weapons'. Among the more bizarre schemes of MKULTRA was the attempt to poison Fidel Castro with the botulinum food-poisoning culture in his milk shake. For the next three years Dr Sidney Gottlieb, the club-footed folk-dancing head (no, really, I'm not making this up!) of the Chemical Division of the CIA's Technical Service Staff, began a programme of funding universities in LSD research. They included Columbia, where Harold Abramson was so enthusiastic in encouraging his colleagues and students to try the new turn-ons that John Marks, author of 'The Search for the Manchurian Candidate', described him as 'one of the first Johnny Appleseeds of LSD'.

In 1969, the US Bureau of Narcotics described the spread of LSD in a special report: '. . . early use was among small groups of intellectuals at large Eastern and West Coast universities. Most often, users have been introduced to the drug by persons of higher status. Teachers have influenced students; upperclasssmen have influenced lowerclassmen.'

One of the first victims of this programme was the tennis pro, Harold Blauer, who was injected with mescaline against his will (and protests) by his civilian psychiatrist in January 1953. Blauer collapsed and died almost immediately. That was three years after the process of making psychedelics respectable had been started by Aldous Huxley's book, 'The Doors of Perception'. General William Creasy, who ordered the programme which killed the tennis star, nevertheless declared afterwards: 'I think the future lies in psycho-chemicals.' The doctors responsible were awarded a further grant of $167,739 to continue their illicit research.

The world's first batch of totally synthetic LSD, produced by the Eli Lilly company in 1953, was handed over in its entirety to the CIA.

In November 1953, a civilian biochemist called Frank Olson, unwittingly drank some Cointreau spiked with LSD at a three-day gathering of scientists organised by the Special Operations Division of the Army Chemical Corps at an ex-Eagle Scout camp at Deep Creek Lodge, Western Maryland – not the first time that subjects were experimented upon without their knowledge or consent, nor the last.

Ten disturbed days later, Olson leapt out of the window of his New York hotel at 2.30 in the morning and crashed to his death on the sidewalk below, possibly the first example of LSD-induced defenestration.

Over the next ten years, various Government agencies experimented upon nearly 1500 subjects and spent hundreds of thousands of dollars on the programme. One of the people turned on to LSD during this programme was Ken Kesey, the Merry Prankster (and author of 'One Flew Over the Cuckoo's Nest'), who got his first tab of acid from Dr Leo Hollister in 1960. As Marks comments in 'The Search for the Manchurian Candidate': '. . . the fact remains that LSD was one of the catalysts of the traumatic upheavals of the 1960s. No one could enter the world of psychedelics without first passing, unawares, through doors opened by the (Central Intelligence) Agency.'

When Frank Zappa suggested to me, years afterwards, that the whole 'mind expansion' hype had been a clever ploy by the CIA on behalf of the entire Western establishment to undermine the potential threat of the emerging youth culture, I thought he was just being paranoid, but I don't think so now.

It has to be remembered that the CIA has had its fingers in financing the heroin trade in South East Asia (even flying supplies out of the opium-growing anti-Vietcong areas during the Vietnam war), the cocaine trade in Bolivia and, today, the heroin produced by the rebels in Afghanistan which has flooded Western Europe, making smack the cheapest high on the street – and the most frequently fatal.

Michael Hollingshead from Leary's Millbrook Centre brought acid into London in mid-1965, and the effect on the music was almost instantaneous. Steve Stollman began organising his Sunday afternoon 'Spontaneous Underground' sessions at the Marquee in February 1966.

'Who will be there?' went the flyer. 'Poets, pop singers, hoods, Americans, homosexuals (because they make up ten per cent of the population), 20 clowns, jazz musicians, one murderer, sculptors,

politicians, and some girls who defy description are among the invited.'
It was hard to say who was a performer and who the audience, since all
the audience were performing madly all the time, and the artists were so
amateurish, in the nicest way, that anyone could get up on stage and jam
with them, and frequently did.

The inspiration was from the West Coast, though Roger Waters says
that no one had then heard of the West Coasters like the Jefferson
Airplane or the Grateful Dead. The Airplane and the Charlatans had
kicked off San Francisco's underground scene with the first Family
Dog dance, 'A Tribute to Dr Strange', at the San Francisco
Longshoreman's Hall on October 16 1965, on the eve of the Berkeley
Vietnam Day march when local Hells Angels were employed by the
Oakland police to beat up the peace protesters – and then went on to
beat up the police, just to show they were impartial.

Light shows had their own superstars, people like Bill Hamm, Henry
Schaeffer, Roger Hillyard, Tony Martin and Ben Van Meter.
Interestingly, at that first Family Dog dance, the lights had played on
the audience rather than the bands. When LSD came to London later
that year, the impedimenta came with it, the strobes, the slides in which
solutions of oil and water paint swirled round, their movement the
result of convection currents from the heat of the projector, all designed
to create the illusion of a good trip.

Bill Hamm had already begun using a light machine to create washes
of colour over the bands the previous summer, but it was Ken Kesey's
Trips Festival over three nights in January, also at the Longshoreman's
Hall, powerfully featured in Tom Wolfe's book 'Kool Aid Acid Test',
but where, according to the late Ralph J. Gleason, nobody actually did
put acid in the Kool Aid.

Gleason's report in the San Francisco Chronicle at the time reported
(after the obligatory references to the weird way people were dressed,
and the young lady who took off her shirt to dance topless): 'There were
five movie screens up on the wall and projections for the flicks and other
light mixes spread around the balcony. A huge platform in the middle of
the room housed the engineers who directed the sound and the lights.
Loudspeakers ringed the hall and were set up under the balcony and in
the entrance.

'A huge pair of red and yellow traffic lights blinked constantly.
Stroboscopic lights set at vantage points beamed down into the crowd
and lissome maidens under them for hours, whirling jewellery. A man
played a penny whistle for one of the dancers.

'On stage a succession of good rock'n'roll bands, the Grateful Dead,
Big Brother and the Holding Company, produced the kind of sonic high
that big bands used to, only the rock bands do it quicker and for more

33

people . . .' Despite this obvious inspiration for what went on at the Marquee on Sundays, the British scene owed as much to the Happening, a typically random access sort of mixed media event that had begun at the Edinburgh Festival a few years previously, shocking the easily shocked British press hacks by the fact that a naked woman actually appeared on stage.

The Floyd appeared for the first time at the Marquee on March 13 1966, when, in addition to the R&B standards they'd been doing since the days of the Abdabs, they also began playing the electronic instrumentals which became their hallmark.

As a result of playing there, the Floyd met the three management moguls of the underground, Peter Jenner, Andrew King and Joe Boyd. Jenner and King went on to manage them (after an earlier attempt to take over the Velvet Underground had been foiled by Andy Warhol), and Boyd produced their first single.

Jenner and King gave them their own thing at the All Saints Hall in Notting Hill, and then when Joe Boyd and John Hopkins (Hoppy) opened the UFO club in the old Blarney Club in Tottenham Court Road, they became the house band. Before that, there'd been an all-night rave to raise money for Hoppy's paper, International Times, where Marianne Faithfull won the 'shortest/barest' prize for coming as a mini-skirted nun, there had been a 'Psychedelia vs Ian Smith' gig organised by the Majority Rule for Rhodesia Committee, and even an Oxfam benefit at the Royal Albert Hall, their biggest gig to date.

Despite the psychedelic tag that attached itself to them, and the dope fumes that arose from the audience whenever they played, the Floyd had only one serious drugs user: Syd.

Ever anxious about the image of his boys, Andrew King distanced them from the psychedelic catchphrase when he spoke to the Sunday Times at the Roundhouse IT benefit: 'We don't call ourselves psychedelic. But we don't deny it. We don't confirm it either. People who want to make up slogans can do it.'

But, in the same article, Roger Waters was quoted as drawing definite parallels between the drug experience and listening to the Floyd: 'It's definitely a complete realisation of the aims of psychedelia. But if you take LSD, what you experience depends entirely on who you are. Our music may give you the screaming horrors or throw you into screaming ecstasy. Mostly it's the latter.'

In 1966 the guru of junk, William S. Burroughs, had equated music with the drugs experience: 'Since junk *is* image the effects of junk can easily be produced and concentrated in a sound and image track – Like this: take a sick junky - Throw blue light on his so-called face or dye it blue or dye the junk blue it don't make no difference and now give him a shot and photograph the blue miracle as life pours back into that walking corpse – That will give you the image track of junk – Now project the blue change onto your own face if you want The Big Fix. The sound track is even easier. – I quote from Newsweek, March 4, 1963 Science section: 'Every substance has a characteristic set of resonant frequencies at which it vibrates or oscillates.' – So you record the frequency of junk as it hits the junk-sick brain cells –

"'What's that? – Brain waves are 32 or under and can't be heard? Well speed them up, God damn it – and instead of one junky concentrate me a thousand – Let there be Lexington and call a nice Jew to run it –'" ('Nova Express')

On the other hand, the band refused to give a benefit for Release, the drug-users legal aid charity, at a time when other prominent rockpersons like Beatle George Harrison were signing their names to £5000 cheques.

Later, when they had signed to EMI, their record company issued an official disclaimer: 'The Pink Floyd does not know what people mean by psychedelic pop and are not trying to create hallucinatory effects on their audiences.'

The drug orientation of Syd Barrett's song, 'Let's Roll Another One' (with lines like 'Tastes right if you eat it right' which Waters admitted were 'very under the arm') was obvious enough to the BBC, who insisted to EMI that it be changed or replaced before 'Arnold Layne', the single of which it was the B-side, could be played. It became 'Candy In a Currant Bun'. This did not stop the Daily Express attacking a proposal to give an Arts Council grant to a Brighton Festival where the band were to play in April '77. 'The Pink Floyd according to some accounts reproduces the sound equivalent of LSD drug visions', the paper's hack complained. 'Its work has been acclaimed by promoters and fans as "psychedelic". And it has taken part in those curious way-out events, simulating drug ecstasies, which are known as "freak outs", in which girls writhe and shriek and young men roll themselves naked in paint or jelly . . . I don't think that the Arts Council (which had promised aid from taxes of up to £5000 for the festival) should put any kind of approving seal on this sort of thing, do you?'

Probably, their association with the rising tide of psychedelia was purely opportunistic, since identification with the pot smokers and acid droppers gave them a ready-made, fiercely loyal constituency. Their commitment to the acid revolution was no greater than that of Bob Dylan to the Greenwich Village folk scene, when that was the only way a young poet could get himself a hearing. Apart from Syd, of course.

At this time, Dave Gilmour's band, Jokers Wild, sometimes shared the bill with the Floyd on their visits to Cambridge.

'Every once in a while we'd find ourselves on the same gig as the Pink Floyd, long before they'd got to having a recording contract, art colleges in London and dances in Cambridge and stuff, because they would come down and play in Cambridge every once in a while, although they were based in London, and we would go and play in London once in a while.

'I would go to some of their gigs and they would come to some of ours so I got to know the others through knowing Syd.

'I lived abroad for most of 1966 and most of 1967, in Spain and France, playing with my band over there. Shortly after I was back in London, I went to a couple of gigs, and at one of them Nick said to me: Keep it under your hat, but would you consider joining the band at some time in the future, because we might need to get someone in?

'I didn't really think any more about it very much.

'Two or three months after that they rang up and said come and join the band and I said OK.

'I actually came back from France at one point, in April or May 1967, because we'd had all our microphones stolen and I came back to buy new microphones in London because you could buy second hand Shures in Lisle St for £7, and new they were 35 quid each in Paris. I came back to buy those and I rang Syd up and spoke to his girlfriend and she said they were in a studio in Chelsea, recording. So I dropped in on them, and they were recording 'See Emily Play'.

'Syd, who had been a friend of mine for years, just looked straight through me, barely acknowledged that I was there. Very weird. That was before their second single had been released.

'I don't think the success that followed would have helped at all. I guess it was a combination of all sorts of things. But I expect that would have happened eventually, regardless.'

Joe Boyd recalls the exact date when he noticed that Syd's contact with the outside world was becoming intermittent. It was a Friday, June 2, 1967, and as usual Joe was keeping the door at UFO, greeting the bands and fans as they came in.

'That was very, very sad,' he recalls. 'The great thing was that Syd was that if there was anything about him that you really remembered it was that he had a twinkle in his eye. I mean he was a real eye-twinkler. He had this impish look about him, this mischievous glint.

'He came by and I said "Hi Syd" and he just kind of looked at me. I looked right in his eye and there was no twinkle, no glint. It was like somebody had pulled the blinds, you know. And it was a real shock.'

When he got on stage, Syd barely played. 'Syd arrived, but his arms hung by his side,' Nick recalled later, but Roger's recollection was that he never came to the gig at all, he made so little contribution, barely touching his guitar.

'He may have been on stage but we really did it without him,' said Roger. 'He just stood there with it hanging round his neck, which was something he was prone to do, and after that we realised we could manage.' The underground press wasn't impressed, however. 'They played like bums,' was the verdict of IT.

Even the TV audience could see that something was happening to Syd: the band's three 'Top of the Pops' appearances saw Syd's Granny Takes a Trip satin and crushed velvet gear getting more and more dishevelled, and for the third appearance, he actually changed out of the smart stuff into scruffy street clothes before he went on the set, and talked about not appearing at all, because John Lennon didn't so why should he?

It was the American tour of November '67 that really sent Syd over the edge. He didn't move his lips when they had to mime to 'See Emily Play' on Dick Clark's 'American Bandstand' TV show, and on the Pat Boone Show he just gave the Mormon crooner a blank stare when he tried to interview him. On the British package tour that followed, a nightmare (Roger's word) on which they opened the second half of a bill that also comprised the Move, Amen Corner, the Nice, Eire Apparent, Outer Limits and topped by Jimi Hendrix, Syd often refused to go on stage, or just wandered away as the curtain went up, and Dave O'List of the Nice had to deputise for him. (A fine instrumentalist, O'List played on Roxy Music's second album in 1977 but hasn't been heard of since.)

On the promo film for 'Apples and Oranges' (November, 1967), Dave Gilmour played guitar and Roger Waters mimed to Syd's voice and in January 1968, Roger Waters asked Dave Gilmour to join the band, which then became a nominal five piece.

'We played I think five or six gigs with five of us, through late January and February '68, I suppose.' Dave told me, many years after. 'Syd accepted it, but there just wasn't any real communication. Syd didn't appear disgruntled, he just didn't communicate about it at all. But then we didn't know what he was thinking about anything any of the time.

'Even in those days recording tended to be a few people playing and then drop-in overdubbing afterwards. There are tracks on 'A Saucerful of Secrets' album that Syd played on and I played on later, a little bit. "Set the Controls for the Heart of the Sun", I think I played a bit on.

'No one knew quite what was going to happen, but I think the original intention was that Syd would sort of step back and be the Brian Wilson character who still wrote stuff but didn't come on the road and appear. I think the management people wanted that, but I think it became fairly obvious that it wasn't going to happen.

'I remember we were going to do a gig in Southampton and I think Roger usually had the car. We had an enormous ancient old Bentley, and Roger would go round and pick everyone up to go to the gig, and he'd picked all of us up, and Syd was the last one to pick up, in Richmond on the way out of London, and someone said "Shall we go and pick up Syd?". And someone else said "Oh no, let's not". And that was it. Just one of those things, it was inevitable.

'Everyone knew Syd's potential and knew how brilliant he was, and the people managing Blackhill Enterprises, they had no real faith in the band being able to make it without him, and being able to do something on their own, and that became a large strain, because there was no real belief in it without Syd. So we departed from them as well.'

Dave and Rick and Roger worked on Syd's two solo albums, but after the third was abandoned as impracticable, they didn't see Syd again until he turned up, uninvited and unexpected, during the making of 'Wish You Were Here' in 1975, which was ironic, since it was inspired in part by him. They didn't recognise the fat skinhead in Terylene trousers, string vest and nylon shirt until another visitor from the past, Andrew King, pointed out who it was.

Today he lives with his mother in Cambridge, and has, it seems, no association with the world of rock.

As such things will, a myth has grown up around Syd Barrett and there are still fan clubs and fanzines devoted to the proposition that he was the most creative thing in Pink Floyd, and that after that it was all downhill.

It's certain that things changed. It's also certain that after his withdrawal others, notably Marc Bolan, went on to make something of a commercial success out of copying the feyness that was for a time his unique contribution to the sound of the underground.

And while they weren't really to find an assured direction until 'Meddle' in 1971 – typically, after a time when they described themselves as 'in acute danger of dying of boredom' – the time of their greatest successes, artistically as well as commercially, must be dated from after Syd's departure.

The decline of psychedelia really coincided with that last, disastrous UFO gig of June '67. The club was moved to the Roundhouse, and Joe brought in Michael X's Black Power strong-arm guys to act as bouncers and keep the mohair-suited post-mods – known to the underground as the Suits – from beating up the hippies on their way in and out of the club, to see if they really believed all that 'peace and love' shit. (Most of them did, and got a horrible kicking as a result of their refusal to retaliate.) As John Lennon said, the dream was over, and its awakening was to the teargas of the May 1968 Paris evenements, the police riot in Chicago during the Democratic Convention, the wipe out of the Black Panthers and the self-destruction of the violent Weathermen (said by many to be funded by the FBI), the rollback of the Red Guards during China's cultural revolution.

Pink Floyd persuaded the Bailiff of the Royal Parks to let them put on a free concert in Hyde Park to promote their new 'Saucerful of Secrets' album, and it established a new tradition of free shows, continued with Blind Faith and the Stones. The album included Syd Barrett's 'Jugband Blues'.

Syd sang:

> *It's most awfully considerate of you to think of me here,*
> *And I'm most obliged to you for making it clear that I'm*
>   *not here . . .*
> *And I'm wondering who could be writing this song.*

PART TWO

The Construction of The Wall

BRICK IV
The Live Shows

So all aboard for the American tour
And maybe you'll make it to the top,
But mind how you go I can tell you 'cos I know
You may find it hard to get off.

Free Four

At best, the Floyd's attitude to touring has always been – how shall we put it? – ambivalent.

That's hardly surprising: it's a rotten job.

Only in one respect, in fact, does the mythical rock lifestyle seem to contain any single recurring factor: not drink, not drugs, not even violence – though there is plenty of this, especially after the bars close and the band is on its way home from the gig.

The most obvious common denominator thrown up by the statistics is not glamorous at all: the sheer, soul-destroying grind of life on the road.

This 'auto-destruct mechanism', as I have called it, was responsible for the most famous deaths of early rock: Hank Williams, Big Bopper, Richie Valens, Patsy Cline, Cowboy Copas, Hawkshaw Hawkins, Carl Perkins' brother Jay (and his manager), Martin Lambell of Fairport Convention, Johnny Kidd, Johnny Horton, Otis Redding, and of course Eddie Cochran, Jim Reeves and Buddy Holly, whose death on February 3 1959 was scheduled by folksinger Don McLean as 'the day the music died'.

Holly's death was undoubtedly due to his horrendous touring schedule. And far from being an easy, get-rich-quick occupation for lazy layabouts, if rock'n'roll was subjected to the attentions of H. M. Factories Act Inspectors, it would undoubtedly be banned.

And also, for an up-and-coming band, with a new attitude to music nurtured by a specific scene, a specific *community* in fact, it was particularly hard to put their noses outside of places where they were already known and respected, where the basic assumptions of their music were known and understood, into the wastelands north of Watford, where the bad old Gradgrind traditions of pop exploitation still held sway.

For in their early days the Floyd were in the only real sense, a folk group.

In December 1970, the perceptive American rock critic Jon Landau – one of the first to realise how debilitating was the idea of rock as art – pointed out what made the rock of the Sixties different from what came before, and from what came after: 'It was a folk music – it was listened to and made by the same group of people. It did not come out of a New York office building where people sit and write what they think other people want to hear. It came from the life experiences of the artists and their interaction with an audience that was roughly the same age.'

Landau was writing about America, in, ironically, Rolling Stone, the single publication most responsible for the rock-as-art theory which has so led the music down a blind alley. The comment applies to Britain at that time, too.

It is one of the hallmarks of a true folk art that doesn't travel well; if it is taken out of its natural environment, like a Norfolk pub singer at the Festival Hall, it either dies, or, to survive, it becomes something entirely different. The Scottish tinker lady, Jeannie Robertson, metamorphosed into a gypsy queen after she had been 'discovered' by the folk scene, was a magnificent person, able to chat on equal terms with the real H. M., and a commanding presence until her death, but far from the gentle singer of the original field recordings.

So with the Floyd, nurtured by the environment of the Tuesday night 'sound/light workshop' at the London Free School in Notting Hill Gate, which grew into UFO in the basement of the old Blarney Club in Tottenham Court Road, and expanded into the Roundhouse, eventually to expire when Joe Boyd called in the hard men of Michael X's black mafia to act as bouncers. They paid their dues, as the saying goes, once they ventured out to tour for what Nick Mason called 'a daily dose of broken bottle'. As Rick Wright commented: 'When we started in UFO it was a beautiful place to play, but when we went outside London nobody wanted to know. People used to throw bottles at us.'

'Actually,' recalls Roger Waters, 'the worst thing that ever happened to me was at the Feathers Club in Ealing, which was a penny, which made a bloody great cut in the middle of my forehead. I bled quite a lot.

'And I stood right at the front of the stage to see if I could see him throw one. I was glowering in a real rage, and I was going to leap into the audience and get him. Happily, there was one freak who turned up who liked us, so the audience spent the whole evening beating the shit out of him and left us alone . . .'

That was at first. Then, when they began to achieve some chart success, with appearances on Top of the Pops, the punters couldn't understand why they wouldn't play their singles, and why they kept on

44

droning on with the 'freak outs', long modal improvisations upon a single chord.

Waters commented: 'We get very upset if people get bored when we're only halfway through smashing the second set. Then all of a sudden they hear 'Arnold Layne' and they flip all over again. It's sad when an audience isn't always with you.

'At the UFO Club in London, the people there are so blasé that they are bored to death with 'Arnold Layne' because it's become a pop song. Yet in other clubs this song is the only song of ours they know and enjoy. Some don't like the song because they think it's a smutty idea for a man to run around pinching clothes from washing lines . . .'

Another time, he said: 'We're being frustrated at the moment by the fact that to stay alive we have to play lots and lots of places and venues that are not really suitable . . .

'We've got a name, of sorts, now among the public, so everybody comes to have a look at us and we get full houses. But the atmosphere in these places is very stale. There is no feeling of occasion.

'There is no nastiness about it, but we don't get re-booked on the club or ballroom circuit.'

What they were thinking of doing, he said, was to take a circus Big Top on the road, and thus export the atmosphere of UFO, where they were truly the 'house band of the underground', in Nick Mason's phrase.

Although I was at UFO dozens of times when Floyd must have played, I can't remember hearing them there specifically. I remember Kenneth Anger's film, 'Fireworks', Jeff Nuttall's People Show, and individual lone groovers like the guy who danced backwards, barging into people and accepted with the sort of amused tolerance I wasn't to experience again until the heady days of early punks pogo-dancing at the Roxy ten years later. I remember the way vertiginously circling sparks of light on the stairway down, reflected from a spot by an old-style ballroom mirror-ball, created a disorientation that was no less powerful for being non-chemical, and therefore legal (a technique the Floyd themselves were to employ on a much larger scale in their Earls Court and Rainbow shows in 1973).

More than this, I remember a melange, a flavour, a totality which was more than just the sum of individual parts, in which music and slides and films and theatrics and audience antics added up to become something quite unique.

'It's got rosier with age,' recalled Nick Mason, 'but there is a germ of truth in it, because for a brief moment it looked as though there might actually be some combining of activities. People would go down to this place, and a number of people would do a number of things, rather than simply one band performing. There would be some mad actors, a couple of light shows, perhaps the recitation of some poetry or verse, and a lot of wandering about and a lot of cheerful chatter going on.'

Dissected, very few of the individual contributions stood up to critical analysis, and the best of them (eg Anger's film) were actually creations of a previous culture; the better they were artistically, the less well they would have submerged themselves into the surrounding ambience of inspired amateurism.

But it is in this multi-media approach that one must search to find the origins of the Floyd show that was to end up with a wall across Earls Court and the Los Angeles Sports Arena.

The following year, the Floyd were using film at an Essex University gig. 'Some bright spark down there had done a film with a paraplegic in London, given this paraplegic a film camera and wheeled him round London filming his view. Now they showed it up on screen behind us as we played.' (Roger Waters)

Films and slides were a natural part of the Spontaneous Underground on Sunday afternoons at the Marquee in Wardour Street, Soho, where the Floyd got their first big start. And while it is true that the purpose of the light shows was to do 'visually what acid rock was doing aurally – expanding the consciousness and reproducing mechanically and harmlessly what LSD, mescalin and other hallucinogens were doing chemically . . . a *safe* turn-on and a short cut to rapture' (Lillian Roxon), it needs to be pointed out that though Pete Jenner labelled Floyd's music 'psychedelic rock' and though they were associated with a scene infatuated with the experiences of acid, the only regular user in the band was Syd Barrett, and we've seen what happened to him!

As Miles comments sadly on the scene at that time: 'A terrifying number of the people I've mentioned are now dead.'

'We are simply a pop group,' said Waters at the time of their second single, 'See Emily Play', was released. 'Because we use light and colour in our act, a lot of people seem to imagine that we are trying to put across a message with some nasty, evil undertones.'

It's generally acknowledged that the real beginning of light shows in Britain can be dated from the time when the Floyd played the London Free School, a church hall in Notting Hill Gate's Powis Gardens where local heads could be advised on housing matters (by Pete Jenner, as it happens), or could groove along to the Sound/Light Workshops organised by Hoppy – John Hopkins, the man who went on to open UFO when the crowds got too big, and without whom the underground more or less collapsed when he was busted for possession.

There was a night when Joel and Toni Brown from Timothy Leary's

Millbrook Centre projected their slides on to the Floyd as they played, though as Nick Mason says, it was more of a gradual process: 'The light show was due to various influences –like someone coming over from the States, heard the band and liked it, and had got a projector and knew how to make a water slide up and did so.'

An important distinction between the British and American attitudes to light shows was the fact that in America the lights were provided by the promoter, or the venue, but in Britain promoters expected the bands to bring their own. This meant it was easier to integrate the lights with the music and the rest of the band's show.

However, no attempt was yet being made to link sound and lights, and indeed that was the whole point: a sort of art by accident was sought, in which random coincidences of sound and image combined to create a unique and unrepeatable audio-visual experience. When that happened it was remarkable, but most of the time it didn't. Nick Mason again: 'The trouble with the projected slides is that everybody tends to ignore the music. If you listen you'll find that it's pretty good – we think so anyway. To us the sound is at least as important as the visual aspect.'

Later Jack Bracelin, (who also ran the 'psychedelic nudist colony' in Watford) and 17-year-old Joe Gannon developed lightshow techniques for the Floyd, partly under the influence of students from Hornsey College of Art where there was a well-developed workshop. Hornsey even provided the lights when the Floyd played the Brighton Festival.

Joe said: 'I design the slides, basing them on my idea of the music. The lights work rhythmically – I just wave my hand over the micro-switches and the different colours flash.'

Roxon puts her finger on an important point when she remarks that quite apart from their drug connotations the sound and lights at psychedelic events both 'involved rock audiences more than they had ever been involved before (a happy extension of the fainting-over-Elvis and jitterbugging-in-the-aisles phenomena of earlier ages)'.

Interestingly, Roger Waters was highlighting specifically this aspect in a 1967 interview: 'What we really want is for complete audience participation. You just don't get it at the Marquee.

'What we want is not just lights flashing on us but on the audience as well – and they should react spontaneously and not simply dance around as they would to normal music. Another good thing would be if we could get a theatre and all the proper equipment.

'We could go two ways as we are at the moment. The one is pure abstraction with the sound and light but the other is complete illustration, pure evocation, like playing to a vase of flowers.'

Rick Wright commented, the year before: 'As we are a comparatively new group and are projecting a really new sound, most people just stand

and listen at first. What we really want is that they should dance *to* the music and *with* the music and so become part of us.'

It was a very Sixties thought: *'I am he and you are we and we are he and all of us together.'* But the desire to break down the barrier – the wall, if you prefer – between Floyd and their audience has continued to be a motivating force behind the band to this very day, ironically leading them to create the very megashows which can only be paid for by putting them into vast stadia and exhibition halls, alienating their audiences from them still further.

In January 1967, classical promoter Christopher Hunt presented the band playing 'music in colour' at the Commonwealth Institute, and four months later he gave them a whole evening at one of London's prime classical venues, the Queen Elizabeth Hall, 'Games for May'.

According to the press publicity: 'The Floyd intend this concert to be a musical and visual exploration – not only for themselves, but for the audience too. New material has been written and will be given for the first time, including some specially prepared four-way stereo' (ie quadraphonic) 'tapes. Visually, the lights men of the group have prepared an entirely bigger-than-ever-before show.

'Sadly, we are not allowed to throw lighting effects as planned on to the external surfaces of the hall, nor even in the foyer. But inside should be enough!'

The band lost money over the concert, since they had to take a week off to get it set up, and the quad didn't quite work, the daffodils they threw to the audience got trodden into the carpets and the soap bubbles they blew into the auditorium left nasty circular marks on the seating where they burst as they landed, so Floyd were banned from the hall for ever more.

Still, Syd Barrett's special song 'Games for May', metamorphosed as their next single 'See Emily Play', and the concert as a whole, were something of a breakthrough, getting them a favourable notice in the Financial Times. Already, however, the Floyd's show was outgrowing the available venues, and Roger Waters thought of borrowing a big top from one of the ailing circuses in Britain – the Billy Smart big top could hold over 5000 people – and using it for tours.

'We want a brand new environment. We'll have a huge tent and go around like a travelling circus. We'll have a huge screen 120 feet wide and 40 feet high inside, and project films and slides.

'We'll play the big cities or anywhere and become an occasion just like a circus. It'll be a beautiful scene. It could even be the salvation of the circus!'

The circus tour never happened, but in June 1968 they played the first Hyde Park free concert with Jethro Tull and Roy Harper – the first rock concert in a Royal park.

Nothing untoward happened – but at later open-air events the Floyd were to utilise effects that would have been impossible indoors, like the two Spitfires that flew over Knebworth in July 1975, themselves presaged by the model 'plane that crashed on stage at the 'Dark Side of the Moon' concert at Earls Court in 1973 (the plane crash was also featured at Knebworth, by the way).

Spring '69 found them back on the South Bank, at the QEH's big brother, the Royal Festival Hall, with 'More Furious Madness from the Massed Gadgets of Auximenes', during the second half of which a silver-sprayed sea monster lumbered around the auditorium, up on to the platform and then backstage.

During July, they were back at the Royal Albert Hall; wood was sawn on stage, someone came on dressed as a gorilla, a cannon was fired and a pink smokebomb exploded during the grand finale.

Of course, these weren't just visual effects: the Floyd were moving into the area of musique concrete – processed real sound effects as the constituents of a piece of music. It was something they had tried when UFO moved to the Roundhouse in September, 1967, and again in 1970, a tape of a child crying was used to tremendous effect during a Hyde Park free concert.

In 1973 they began experimenting with an entirely 'musique concrete' album, which was abandoned after three tracks had been recorded.

'We used rubber bands,' recalled Gilmour, 'we actually built a long stretched rubber band thing, about two feet. There was a G clamp one end fixing it to a table and another G clamp at the other end fixing it to a table. There was a cigarette lighter under one end for a bridge and there were a set of matchsticks taped down the other end. You stretch it and you can get a really good bass sound.'

'We used aerosol sprays and pulling rolls of Sellotape out to different lengths. The further away it gets the note changes.'

On abandoning the album, Roger Waters said: 'It seemed like a good idea at the time, but it didn't really come together.'

By then, a similar technique had already been one of the talking points of their first really successful album, 'Atom Heart Mother', on which 'Alan's Psychedelic Breakfast' – Alan was presumably Alan Parsons, one of the two engineers on the album – utilised actuality sound, though not very successfully, as the band agrees.

Nick Mason: 'It's quite interesting, insofar as although we've all agreed that the piece didn't work, in some ways the sound effects are the strongest part. It was a fantastic idea but because of the rush it didn't work properly.'

Dave Gilmour: '"Alan's Psychedelic Breakfast" never achieved what it was meant to. It was meant to be how it should've been. It was a bit of a throw-together, in fact the most throw-together thing we've ever done.'

Rick Wright: '"Alan's Psychedelic Breakfast" we tried on our English tour' [in 1972] 'and it didn't work at all so we had to give it up. None of us liked doing it anyway and we didn't like it on the album – it's rather pretentious, it doesn't do anything. Quite honestly, it's a bad number.

'A similar idea in that idiom we did at the Roundhouse another time I thought was much better. Practically on the spot we decided to improvise a number where we fried eggs on stage and Roger threw potatoes about and it was spontaneous and it was really good.

'"Alan's Psychedelic Breakfast" was a weak number.'

Roger Waters: 'We did that in a fantastic rush, didn't we?'

By the time of the 'Atom Heart Mother' tour they were beginning to make enough money on their record sales to afford to lose £2000 a night on their concerts – and more, in America.

An idea of the sort of costs involved even then can be obtained from the list of equipment stolen from the group in New Orleans in 1970: a 4000-watt PA, two drum kits, 12 speakers, electric organ, four guitars, five echo units, microphones and miles of lead, valued $40,000. Today, you could add two or three zeroes at the end of that figure.

Meanwhile, Nick Mason was saying: 'We've always had this bigger concept in mind; there have always been big plans. But it's only this year, really, that we've become financially stable so we can start organizing things to suit us rather than let it go on round us.

'The thing to do is to really move people – to turn them on, to subject them to a fantastic experience, to do something to stretch their imagination.'

What this was to mean was seen – and heard – in February 1972, when the band premiered 'Dark Side of the Moon' at the Rainbow for four nights. It took four roadies six hours to move in the nine tons of equipment, and 12000 people saw it. 'Dark Side' is a remarkable work by any standards, but remarkable in this context for the way in which natural sounds play a musical role, whether it be the cash registers ringing up in 7/4 time in 'Money', or the terrifying snatches of conversation that emerge from the music like a sort of subversive commentary, culminating in the chilling final words of the piece: 'There is no dark side of the moon. Matter of fact, it's all dark.'

Many of the speech sounds on the record come from Roger the Hat, the famous roadie, who recalled with great glee the last time he'd thumped someone, administering a 'short, sharp shock' (Government ministers will recognize the expression) to a road user who'd endangered, in his opinion, his truck. It is Roger the Hat whose stoned, maniacal laughter makes 'Brain Damage' so chilling, the rising cadence of the laughter at the words *The lunatic is in my head* performing a musical purpose, as well as contributing to the general impact of the work's climax.

The 'Dark Side' concerts also marked the maturity of the Floyd's use of projected images, especially by the time they were beginning to phase the piece out of their programme at the Wembley concerts of November 1974, when they utilized their huge circular screen for the first time, projecting film of Edward Heath apparently singing along with 'Brain Damage'.

They also had a remarkable 'money' sequence, utilizing shots of coins, bank notes, gold records and copies of 'Dark Side of the Moon'. They had spent ten days filming at Elstree to get the images right, and they had invested a lot of money in new equipment, so that even though they sold out, the $100,000 investment in the tour meant it had to lose money. Rick Wright said: 'It was hard work for Roger, Nick and Arthur Max, the sound engineer, but it's still not right. I think we are still at the experimental stage in finding out what visuals work and which don't – even after all these years.

'It's so easy to have a film that is distracting and, of course, I've never any idea of what the effect of the film is, I'm always on stage playing.

'People always expect the Floyd to come up with something different, new and better when it comes to visuals, and it's very difficult to keep thinking of new ideas.'

Of course, quite apart from their own experience in the use of film, going back to their very earliest gigs, the Floyd had been utilized by many film-makers who felt (usually correct) that they could provide the necessary musical backdrop to contemporary scenes in films like Peter Whitehead's 'Tonite Let's Make Love in London'. Barbet Schroeder's 'More', or, most notoriously, Antonioni's 'Zabriskie Point', where the director rejected most of their music.

Antonioni did use a variation on 'Careful With that Axe Eugene', called 'Come in 51, Your Time Is Up', for the concluding explosion sequence, where the slow-motion shots of debris flying through the air really work as an appropriate combination of sound and image, though not as beautifully as George Greenhough's marriage of 'Echoes' with slow-motion footage shot by a surfer going through the 'curl' of a wave on the California coastline in 'Crystal Voyager', probably the best surfing film ever made.

'Echoes' also opens and closes Adrien Maben's film 'Pink Floyd at

Pompeii', premiered at the Edinburgh Festival in September 1972 and 'banned' by the Rank Organisation from being shown at the Rainbow in November the same year, for the implausible reason that the Rainbow's lease (it was an ex-cinema) forbade its competing with Rank Cinemas, none of which had evinced any interest in showing the movie.

Despite what Waters calls 'rather Top of the Popsy shots of us walking around the top of Vesuvius' and a naïve obsession with high tech (i.e. lots of shots of the backs of speaker stacks, stencilled PINK FLOYD (LONDON), it's a fairly superior concert movie, shot in a Roman amphitheatre with no audience, which continues to be interesting enough to be reissued in stereo videocassette and videodisc formats, though without the interview footage which Fred Dellar, author of 'NME Guide to Rock Cinema', considered 'hilariously naïve' but which Waters felt made it 'much more lively', cutting it from 85 to 59 minutes. In addition, the movie originally included some studio footage of the band working on 'Us and Them', a song written for 'Zabriskie Point' but eventually used in 'Dark Side of the Moon'.

During the 'Dark Side' tour, Roger Waters began putting together the ideas which were to surface, two albums later, first as 'Animals' and then as 'The Wall', scribbling down seemingly disconnected thoughts in big A4 sketchbooks, with no idea how they were going to work out: 'a real stadium full of real pigs . . . the building of The Wall . . . inflating costumes . . . tiny stage . . . eaten by pigs . . .'

One page was headed: 'Animals, film, 90-minute feature'.

'Animated . . . animals wearing our faces . . . us wearing blank faces . . . animal faces . . . applauding, baying . . .

'Pigs selling fireworks, dogs selling T-shirts . . . arrival of audience . . . group consumed by things . . .'

'Wall of dreams . . .

'The Wall with ducks across it . . . old man scavenging . . . and this guitar . . . shitting ducks . . .

'As long as I get bigger I feel OK . . . nobody can hurt me behind my Wall . . . muslin wall . . .

'Second half . . . optimism . . . pessimism . . . fear . . . building the Wall . . . co-operation breeds progress, competition breeds decay.'

But first there was to be 'Wish You Were Here', a work which delves deeper into the themes of alienation which Waters had begun to explore as long ago as 'Echoes', a piece from the old days which persisted in their repertoire much longer than most of the other old material.

In the concerts, animated film was used to tremendous effect to underline the significance of songs like 'Welcome to the Machine': a mechanical, reptilean metal dinosaur, clambered over a nuked-out, lunar landscape.

Rick Wright explained at the end of 1974: 'We always like to write numbers, go on the road with them and record them later. We did this with 'Dark Side of the Moon' and we think it's easily the best way to go about it. A number changes so much when we do it live over a long period. 'Shine On' has changed a lot since we started already.

'We always play heavier when we don't know songs so well. When we first performed 'Dark Side' it was heavier and harsher than it is now. As we get to know a song better, we tend to play it quieter.'

The increasing complexity of the show meant that they were more susceptible to equipment failure, especially at the beginning of a tour. Ironically, this was usually the concert reviewed by the critics, and the band were experiencing the irritation of receiving high praise for what they regarded as a bum gig – only marginally better than getting a bad review for a good performance.

Dave Gilmour said after a malfunction-plagued concert at Wembley on November 14, 1974: 'I was definitely dispirited. It gets very depressing when you're fighting against odds like dud equipment. Energy soon flags. We weren't pleased to do an encore because we didn't deserve it. 'I'm not interested in disguising my feelings on stage with showbiz devices. I've seen hundreds of bands on stage do that. Does anybody respect them? When I'm standing there I'm conscious of trying to give the most I can.'

Interestingly, though the critics were at this stage still sufficiently bedazzled by the technology to ignore (or, probably, be unaware of) the longueurs, the fans were not so blind and deaf. One wrote angrily to MM: 'I came away from Wembley bitterly disappointed. To me, Floyd were an unbelievable flop. Whatever happened to the much publicised quad sound? I, like many others around me, had a job to believe they were using their normal quota of equipment, the tone and volume were appalling.

'The singing was atrocious, it was never in tune, nor was the harmonising. The empty spaces between numbers and the failing of mikes and other pieces of equipment reminded me more of a nervous pub group doing a quick stand-in.'

In the same issue, however, Michael Oldfield (the journalist, not the guitarist; he was later the editor, then the chief sub), was calling it 'Floyd's Finest Hour'.

'. . . after years of the Pink Floyd's existence, in which they've hardly changed their musical ends or ideals,' he wrote, 'some people still insist on seeing them in terms of yer average rock 'n' roll band. They can't accept that the tons of equipment, the lights, the films and the effects are carted around at considerable expense not for the purpose of providing cheap theatrics, but to heighten the effect of their music . . .

'. . . The performance of 'Dark Side of the Moon' on their current tour is the best yet; fine music counterpointed by a magnificent film which pushes the actual appearance of the musicians on stage even further into the background.

'Some critics won't like that, of course. They still want to see spotlights pinpointing the four musicians ripping off heavy blues solos . . .'

The following year was split between touring and recording 'Wish You Were Here', of which Roger said many years later: 'It could equally have been called 'Wish *We* Were Here', because in the band we were going through one of our communication troughs at that point, a divergence of opinion about what we were doing, what records should be about.'

That was the tour that reduced Derek Meddings to a shadow of his former self when he took some time off from James Bond stunts to mastermind the Floyd's flashes and bangs:

'He was a sort of bouncy, fit, special effects man from the film industry at the beginning of the tour and at the end he was a broken shell. He just hadn't understood how physically demanding it was to be part of a group on the road. He never did another tour. He went back into the film industry.' (Roger Waters)

Meddings worked with the Floyd again briefly, concocting the 'stab-in-the-back' dagger on the sleeve of 'The Final Cut'.

Compared with members of the band, though, Meddings had an easy time. Between January and July they spent over 30 days recording and played 25 North American dates at places like the San Francisco Cow Palace, the Denver Coliseum, and the San Diego Sports Arena, as well as the Knebworth Festival on July 5.

It was during this tour that Roger became so aware of the alienation between the band and their audience that he began thinking of building a physical wall across the front of the stage. 'I found it very unpleasant, unnerving and upsetting. People con each other that there is no wall between performer and audience, so I thought it would be good to build one of black polystyrene or something.'

Elsewhere I have examined the fickleness of the music media towards major artists, and towards the Floyd in particular, but it has to be admitted that there is a distance which the band puts between itself and the press which is itself responsible for some of the misconceptions of the music press reporters.

At Knebworth in July 1975, for instance, MM writer Chris Charlesworth confessed himself disappointed by the opening acts, particularly by Roy Harper, whose appearance on stage was delayed, as he reported, by 'a tantrum when he discovered that his chauffeur-driven Rolls-Royce had driven away with his stage clothes in the boot'.

The incident, and the way Charlesworth reports it became lodged in Roger Waters' consciousness to emerge as one of the climactic points of 'The Wall' several years later.

Harper is a long-time friend of the band, and had co-starred with the Floyd and Jethro Tull at the first Hyde Park free concert in June 1969. Later, he was actually brought in to sing 'Have a Cigar' on the 'Wish You Were Here' album, when Waters decided his voice wasn't up to it. In return, sort of, Dave Gilmour played on Harper's 'Unknown Soldier' album, played in the band on the album's promotional tour, and co-wrote one of the album's best songs, 'Short and Sweet', which he also performed himself on his own solo album. The stormy petrel of the British folk scene, self-styled 'one man rock 'n' roll band', disciple of Nietzsche and opponent of militant feminism, Harper was at the time one of the darlings of the British music press – needless to say, he has since become a non-person. Harper had just produced what is possibly one of his best albums, 'H.Q.', and it had got nowhere. Knebworth presented him with a challenge – and an opportunity to use the occasion to turn the Floyd's audience on to something quite different from the semi-acoustic work with which they probably associated Harper.

'I was going to do something special for the 20,000 in the crowd that could see me. I had a whole thing worked out, a few gags here and there, I'd dressed myself like a space cowboy almost.

'We got there on the day and I guess it was the straw that broke the camel's back, the very first thing that happened was that the whole of my stage gear got nicked. I got incredibly depressed.

'I went into one of the empty caravans. I sat there for a couple of minutes. I just thought: *Release!*

'I got up and I started to smash the caravan. I smashed the whole of the interior of that caravan. After about five minutes of really letting loose I came out quite hurt. I wasn't caring about physical damage to me. The more physical damage happened to me, the more damage happened to the caravan.

'After five minutes I just happened to look out of the window. There was about 150 people in a semi-circle around the caravan all looking at it. It was like there was a touch-line 25 yards away, they were all round it. There was a game taking place.

'After that I had to laugh. I carried on smashing the caravan up but I had to laugh then because I saw the ridiculousness. I saw actually what was going on. I saw myself in a mirror.

'I think the Floyd had to pay three or four thousand quid for the caravan. It was pretty wrecked. There was a bottle through every window.'

After the film of 'The Wall' in which Bob Geldof as Pink does an equally efficient job of wrecking a hotel room, I asked Roger Waters if the Harper incident was its inspiration.

'Oh, that's right,' he recalled. 'I'd forgotten about that. I remember that now. It's quite possible that that incident has been lurking somewhere in my sub-conscious.'

On the other hand, wrecking of hotel rooms *has* become something of a rock 'n' roll cliché. The Who's Keith Moon was notorious for it; and even so sedate a band as Steeleye Span, the folk rock outfit, had one member who specialized in it. In one West Coast hotel, a famous band's roadies got superglue and turned an entire room upside-down, fixing carpets, beds, TV, telephone and everything to the ceiling, with the ceiling light fixed to the floor, as an expensive surpise for the chamber maids in the morning. So it's as likely to be the result of exultant high spirits, often the manic 'high' that comes from speeding drugs like amphetamine or cocaine, as the deep depression it symbolises in 'The Wall'.

Meanwhile, however, at Knebworth the show went on. Charlesworth wasn't too impressed by the Floyd's first half, given over to their new songs, and felt that the replay of 'Dark Side of the Moon' in the second 'limped rather than romped to its usually stunning climax.'

He devoted most of his comments, apart from acknowledging the playing on 'Any Colour You Like' as 'a spectrum of ideas not contained on the record', to the special effects, to justify the headline: PLANE SAILING FOR FLOYD.

In many ways, Knebworth was the apogee of the Floyd's stage show, with two Spitfires flying over the open-air ground at the opening, a plane crashing on to the stage, flares, rockets, and films combining to produce a launch for 'Wish You Were Here' that concealed the fact that the band was on the verge of breaking up, which is why they didn't perform in public again until January 1977, when they kicked off the 'Animals' tour at Dortmund's vast Westfalenhalle. The first of 46 dates in six months, before a total of nearly 2½ million people.

That was the tour with the inflatable flying pig, a demonic-looking construct with glaring eyes, whose oppressive presence Roger Waters rather defused with his cheerful question to the audiences: 'D'you like our pig?' But the humour had vanished by the time of the notorious incident during the final gig at the Olympic Stadium, Montreal, when Waters found himself spitting in the face of an over-enthusiastic fan.

The event had taken over.

The Equipment and Technical Riders for the promoters' contracts for that 1977 European tour is an awesome document:

'1. (a) . . .This stage should be a scaffold platform of interlocking tubular structure capable of sustaining up to 500kg of equipment per square metre. The surface of the finished deck should be fireproofed plywood, stable and have no flexibility and be level with no irregularities to ensure adequate support to equipment which is highly sensitive to vibration and movement . . .

'The sides of the stage platform should be covered with matte black material wherever visible by the audience. A security barrier 1 metre20 high is to be erected around the stage at a distance of between 1m and 1m50.

'The stage must be strengthened to support the weight of the hydraulic towers (approximately 5,000kg each).

'The optimum stage height required is 1m85 . . .

'(b) The projection tower must be of an extremely stable construction, capable of supporting a highly sensitive cine projector and other delicate equipment of approximate total weight 750kg . . .

'Platform dimensions are 4 metres by 4 metres at an exact height of 5m40 above stage level. Provision must be made to lift the projector and associated equipment on to the platform . . .

'The projector dimensions are 2m20 in height, 1m20, wide, 1m80 long and 500kg in weight.

'The tower is to be equipped with a 90cm safety rail on four sides and a 2m20 rail on the back and sides. For those venues where the projector is to be raised through the tower itself, the structure of the tower is to be continued to a height of 4 metres above the platform level, and topped with a rigid steel joist and block and fall or chain hoist. There should be no structural uprights on the front of the tower above platform level.

'(c) Quadraphonic speaker platforms

'Three scaffolding towers will be required of rigid construction . . .

'These towers should be 2 metres high by 4 metres long by 2 metres deep, with 3 metres overhead clearance. The area directly below these towers will contain highly valuable equipment, so each tower should be surrounded by the 1m20 security barriers.

'(d) An area no less than 6 metres wide by 5 metres deep on the ground floor audience level at the exact centre of the house, ie equidistant from stage front and house rear, left and right, must be reserved for the sound and light mixers. Contained in this area is to be a platform 5m50 wide by 1m20 deep and with a height of 75cm. This platform must be able to support equipment weighing 500kg. Behind this platform, seating must be supplied for Pink Floyd's technicians who will be operating the sound and lighting for the duration of the concert. It is essential that the whole area is surrounded by a secure barrier (1m 20 high)...

'2.   The area above the stage must be clear of any hanging obstruction to a height of 15 metres to allow clearance for equipment to be flown over the stage...

'6 metres from the front of the projection tower, we require facilities for flying a circular 9 metre projection screen. The screen frame and material weigh approximately 250 kg...

'5.   The optimum follow-spot requirement is as follows: Eight Super Trouper follow-spots must be provided for each performance no later than 14.00 on the day of the performance and should be equipped with the following Roscolene filters:–

841 Surprise pink
817 Deep golden amber
839 Rose purple
866 Deep urban blue
823 Medium red
877 Medium blue green

'Eight qualified and experienced operators, who must be able to understand simple lighting cues in English, should be called no later than half an hour prior to the time of the performance...

'7.   Pink Floyd require access for equipment trucks at 8.00 on the day of the set-up. Sixteen stage hands should be provided...

'8. (a) Two fork lift units with two experienced drivers should be provided for the load-in (8.00) and load-out of all Pink Floyd equipment. Both should be in good working order.

'(b) Two motorised trolley units suitable for interior use must also be provided...

'POWER REQUIREMENTS

'1: PROJECTOR

'3 phase 4 wire and earth (each phase 240 volts); 60 amps per leg; brought to base of projector tower.

'2: QUAD STATIONS

'The three 'audience' stations each require:– Single phase plus earth; 60 amps; 240 volts.

'3: STAGE

'Single phase plus earth; 200 amps; 240 volts; brought on stage (stage right).

'4: LIGHTS

'3 phase 4 wire plus earth (each phase 240 volts); 200 amps per leg; brought to below the stage (stage right).

'5: HYDRAULIC MOTORS

'3 phase 4 wire and earth (each phase 240 volts); 60 amps per leg; brought to below the stage (stage right...'

Of course, the more complex the technology, the more things can go wrong. At Dortmund, the smoke machine wasn't powerful enough, so in Frankfurt they used a smoke bomb, which filled the exhibition hall with clouds so thick that no one could see the stage.

Angry fans started throwing bottles; one hit sound engineer Brian Humphries on the head, the other struck Nick Mason's double drumkit, and splashed its contents in his face.

And when you realize that there are 20,000 soldered joints in the entire system, it is easy to see how much midnight oil has to be burned to trace a fault, especially when, as in London, local authority 'jobsworths' had worked diligently, earthing everything 'for safety' when no one was looking, and in fact creating a multiplicity of earth loops which add up to an enormous hum.

'I'm the one who was most affected,' Gilmour complained to me after the first night, 'because I'm the one with all the foot switches and special effects. They steam in at the last moment, when you are hoping to get the show on for 8,000 people who have paid their money, and then they do things like that without even telling you.

'After all the trouble and expense we go to, they fuck you up.'

Not everyone realized the amount of time and money that were spent on ensuring the best possible performance. For instance, every drum in Nick Mason's kit was individually miked, and each signal went through an individual noisegate triggered only when that drum was hit, so the usual sound spillage which means that everything else on stage tends to be picked up by the drum mikes, muddying up the sound, is avoided, and the drum sound is crisp and clean.

As I wrote at the time: 'It all adds up to the clearest sound I have ever heard in a hall this size, so if anyone tells you that concerts in these big clangy barns have got to suffer the sort of sound you usually get at Olympia or Earls Court, just tell 'em they're wrong.'

The special effects tended to be Roger Waters' ideas.

At one of the Wembley rehearsals, I heard him instructing the crew: 'I want the smoke to begin at the words "all tight lips and cold feet" at the beginning of the second verse of "Pigs". And I want as much smoke as you can give me. I don't want the audience to see the pig until the loud solo from Dave that comes after the verse.'

And while many critics objected to the fact that Waters wore headphones all the time, this was so he could hear the 'click track' on the soundtrack of the film, allowing the band to play in sync with the projected image – for most of the sound at such times is still live, and not recorded as many seem to think. Ironically, the very technology designed to bring audience and artist closer together was driving them farther apart.

This division was dramatised in 'The Wall', the most grandly conceived and most powerful Floyd work ever, and arguably the most important project in the history of the idiom. Though Roger had acquired a fierce hatred of touring one-night stands, he found 'The Wall' much less distressing, because he was more in control.

Both he and Gilmour have a high regard for it. Said Roger: 'If you look at the work that we've done together, a lot of it's very good. "The Wall" is very good, it's a *very good* record, I think. Dave's contribution is very important.

'Not just his guitar playing, but a couple of really good tunes that he wrote for "The Wall". I'm not belittling his guitar-playing. His guitar-playing is fantastic, he's a very under-rated guitar player in my opinion.'

Dave actually described the show as fun: 'I enjoy doing concerts. I don't enjoy all of the other trappings that go along with it. I'm happy to live with them, myself.

'The "Wall" show, for a number of performances, was really good fun. I mean, obviously it's a very, very theatrical show, there's not much room for expressing oneself personally just as a musician playing. There's no room for going off at tangents at any time. I was very happy with that. I don't mind that at all, for a while. But after a while it's like a piece of theatre and you all do your part and you do your best to do it well and that's about as far as it goes. But it was terrific fun.'

A year later, Dave was still singing its praises, though his words were beginning to sound more like an obituary as he cast his mind back over the years: 'There is a lot of good solid stuff there that I am proud of, yes. Really, for me, from the "Meddle" album through the "Wall" album, I'm very happy with all of it. There's things on all those records that I like a lot. And of course there are loads of other things, loads of tours, performances and gigs we've done that also leave a very satisfying feeling in one. The "Wall" shows in particular were terrific fun and were quite an event, I think.

'All the other tours as well, I've got a great fondness for, for different reasons. Some of them were not as big as the "Wall" show – *none* of them were as big as the "Wall" show – but at some of them the music was played with a lot of fire and enthusiasm.'

After 'The Wall', there was talk of another Floyd tour, though with communication within the band being almost as bad as it was at the time of 'Wish You Were Here' and Rick Wright having silently departed because, in Waters' own words, 'our paths were no longer parallel enough', it seemed unlikely.

Dave was more blunt: 'Rick's leaving is not really leaving. He got the boot, you know, because he wasn't contributing in any way to anything. Now, I argue, vehemently, about a lot of things with Roger about the way we want to do things, but I still see it as being something that I contribute to in a large way, and that I enjoy contributing to in a large way, certainly up to and including "The Wall".'

At one stage I was given a possible date for concerts of November 1983, later withdrawn.

Waters said they would definitely not be performing 'The Wall' again.

'I can't imagine that,' he said, 'the aggravation of getting it together. You never know. We won't be certain about that for another few years when one will know that everything has rotted and all the machinery is rusty. If you haven't seen it again in the next five years then you'll know you're not going to, because everything will have been stolen or rusted away, the cardboard will all be soggy.

'It's not something that I'd care to do again, but it's something that I'm glad to have been part of.'

According to Dave, the tour plan was scuppered by Roger, and he sounds very bitter about it: 'He changed his mind and said he didn't want to. We did have a plan to try, it was all costed out, managers and people went away and told us where we could do it and what we could do and how much money we could make and all that sort of stuff, but Roger just a few weeks ago said "Forget it". It's a very hard thing, because for years and years we've always done things like touring on the basis of if everyone agrees then we could do it, and if anyone actually doesn't want to do it then we just don't do it.

'Now everyone else does want to do it, and Roger still sort of maintains that same option that we've all been happy to live with in the past, so we still go along with it. You can't force people to go out and do a tour when they don't want to, especially you can't force Roger to and he's fundamental to it.'

By 1984, both were touring, but promoting individual solo albums, not Floyd collaborations. Dave's tour was fairly low-key compared with the Floyd megashows, but Roger's continued in the old tradition, with a powerful series of back projections designed by Gerald Scarfe.

The first half was a series of Floyd favourites, ranging from 'Set the Controls for the Heart of the Sun' to 'The Gunner's Dream' from 'The Final Cut'. After a second half devoted to the new solo album, he concluded with 'Brain Damage', with the familiar footage of Edward Heath et al.

I expressed some surprise to Roger that, hating touring as he did, and having blown out the last Floyd tour, he had returned to the road.

'We were never going to tour, anyway,' he said. 'We might have done one gig for a TV simulcast, but I got involved with "The Pros and Cons of Hitch Hiking" and I thought I might well do something theatrical with it. I had a feeling at the time that I would try and organise it into theatre, I mean small theatre, rather than big rock theatre, but in the end, maybe because I feel confident about doing rock theatre and also because Eric Clapton was pushing me to go on the road, I decided to go the Earl's Court/Westfalen Halle route.

'In '77 I swore I would never do stadium shows again as they had turned me into an animal, and I never will. But this tour is completely different from the '77 Floyd tour.

'This is very much more like doing the "Wall" shows. They were tough, even though they were only in sports arenas, and I carried the main burden of responsibility. There was much more to go wrong in that show than there is in this one.

'This one is cleverer, it's just as effective but simpler to put up and knock down.'

BRICK V
The Singles

With the exception of 'Scarecrow', 'Another Brick in the Wall, Part Two' and 'Not Now John', the 'Relics' compilation, and in America, where singles are habitually taken off albums, the Floyd have kept their singles and albums rigidly separate.

Indeed, their attitude to singles and the whole 'Top of the Pops' charts promo schmeer, made them one of the first of the 'album bands' and laid the basis for later rock groups like Led Zeppelin, who were able to build a whole career without ever recording a single.

Strangely, though, when an ageing hippy refers nostalgically to the golden age of the Floyd, it is usually 'Arnold Layne' and 'See Emily Play' he is referring to, numbers which were rarely performed live, and which were dropped from the repertoire as soon as possible.

'Arnold Layne' (Barrett)
'Candy and a Currant Bun' (Barrett)
Prod Joe Boyd, eng John Woods, rec Sound Techniques, Feb 27 1967, rel Mar 11 1967

'Arnold Layne', their first single, was a song about a transvestite who stole women's clothes from washing lines in Cambridge: *Arnold Layne had a strange hobby, collecting clothes/Moonshine, washing line . . ./ Distorted view/See-thru baby blue/He dug it, oh . . . oh! . . .*

This was three years before the Kinks' 'Lola' had managed to smuggle a similar theme past the Mrs Grundies of the BBC, who'd been too busy getting them to change the name of a branded soft drink to 'Cherry Cola' to notice the actual subject matter of the song.

At first the BBC moguls' wrath was reserved for the B-side, originally 'Let's Roll Another One', rewritten as 'Candy and a Currant Bun', whereupon the Beeb's attention switched to the subject of the A-side, so

63

they never played it. Nor did the pirate radio stations, Radios London and Caroline, but it still got into the charts, coming in at 41 on April 1, rising to 20 by April 22, but dropping out the following week. The Dubliners' 'Seven Drunken Nights' jumped from 14 to 11 that week (partly because they didn't refuse to pay off Caroline, as Floyd had done), and Sandie Shaw's 'Puppet on a String' jumped to number one. Weird things happened in the charts those days! Complaints that the song was 'smutty' upset Roger Waters: 'The attitude is the type of thing which leads us to the kind of situation which the song is about. It is a real song about a real subject. It isn't just a collection of words like 'love', 'baby' and 'dig' put to music, like the average pop song . . . If we can't write and sing songs about various forms of human predicament then we might as well not be in the business.'

Syd Barrett, who wrote it, explained: 'I was at Cambridge at the time I started to write the song. I pinched the line about "moonshine washing line" from Rog, our bass guitarist, because he has an enormous washing line in the back garden of his house. Then I thought, Arnold must have a hobby, and it went from there.

'Arnold Layne just happens to dig dressing up in women's clothing. A lot of people do – so let's face up to reality.'

According to Roger Waters, 'Both my mother and Syd's mother had students as lodgers, because there was a girl's college up the road. So there were constantly great lines of bras and knickers on our washing lines, and Arnold, or whoever he was, had bits and pieces off our washing lines. They never caught him. He stopped doing it after a bit – when things got too hot for him. Maybe he's moved to Cherry Hinton or Newnham possibly.'

In the song, Arnold is described as 'a nasty sort of person' who gets caught: *They gave him time/Doors clang chain gang/He hates it, poor Arnold Layne/Arnold Layne, don't do it again.*

But as Nick Mason remembers it, the band didn't want it as their first single: 'By the time "Arnold Layne" was released, we had already progressed and changed our ideas about what a good hit record should be. We tried to stop it being released but we couldn't.'

'See Emily Play' (Barrett)
'Scarecrow' (Barrett)
Prod Norman Smith, eng John Woods, rec Sound Techniques, May 23 1967. rel June 16 1967

Musically, 'Emily' was not so much a precursor of what was to come, as one of the last of the string of soppy flower power songs like the Move's 'I Can Hear the Grass Grow' and the Flowerpot Men's 'Let's Go to San Francisco'. The future was much more to do with the Beatles' 'Penny Lane/Strawberry Fields For Ever' single, Hendrix' 'Purple Haze' and the stream-of-consciousness verbal doodling of Procol Harum's Bach rip-off 'Whiter Shade of Pale'.

In fact, the Floyd's next single, 'See Emily Play', with lines like *Put on a gown that touches the ground/Float on a river for ever and ever*, Emily, now reads like a Zappa parody fit to go into 'We're Only In It For The Money' alongside the immortal *Diamonds on velvets on goldens on vixen/On comet and cupid on donner and blitzen/On up and away and afar and a go-go/Escape from the weight of your corporate logo!*

Miles says that 'See Emily Play' was a reworking of the theme song for 'Games for May', the Floyd's Queen Elizabeth Hall concert of May 12 1967, but I seem to remember them playing 'Emily' at the '14-Hour Technicolor Dream' in aid of International Times on April 29. This is confirmed by 'The Illustrated Rock Almanac' (edited by Miles, as it happens!), so it's possible they were two alternative sets of lyrics to the same tune. No recordings of 'Games for May' seem to exist to check our memories.

'Layne' had been produced by Joe Boyd, but when Beecher Stevens signed the band to EMI for a £5000 advance, the company hadn't yet come to terms with the independent producer concept (George Martin was accepted as an independent after he left the staff in 1965 only because he and the Beatles had become inseparable). Boyd was given the elbow, and Norman Smith, another staff producer, was given the Floyd.

Boyd recalled later: 'It was a bit galling at the time to have Norman Smith suddenly appointed as their record producer and I remember I was very conscious of the fact that they went in and spent a great deal of money and time, a great deal of EMI's money and a great deal of EMI's studio time, trying to get the sound I got down at Sound Techniques on "Arnold Layne" for their follow-up, and ended up having to go down to Sound Techniques and getting the same engineer and recording at Sound Techniques in order to get the same sound.'

According to Beecher Stevens, the reason he wanted his own man at the helm was that he thought the Floyd were rather strange and would need some keeping in hand.

Speaking to Michael Wale, Roger Waters described it as 'a bloody stupid deal', but as Boyd says, 'if the group felt strongly enough that they wanted me to be their record producer they would have insisted on me to EMI'.

As a pop single, 'Emily' is certainly more commercial than 'Arnold Layne', even putting the latter's general weirdness on one side: 'Emily' is hardly about 'The human predicament', in Water's words. 'Layne' gets to grips with a real situation, even if it delivers no great revelations about the human psyche, whereas 'Emily' doesn't make any such demand on its listeners.

The B-side, 'Scarecrow', was later to be the penultimate song on their first album, the first and only time they included an already released single track on an otherwise original LP, although very occasionally (twice, as it happens) they have put out album tracks subsequently as singles.

'Apples and Oranges' (Barrett)
'Paint Box' (Wright)
Prod Norman Smith, rec EMI, Abbey Road, Nov 2 1967, rel Nov 18 1967

By the time of their third single, in November, Syd Barrett was withdrawing from reality and from an active role in the Floyd, so for the first time another member, Rick Wright, contributes a song, though it's a B-side. Again Syd's song is a vignette, and even less happens: going shopping and bumping into a female acquaintance. *Cornering me as she trips up the street to see the people/She's on time again and/Then I catch her by the eye, then I have to stop and think what a funny thing to do 'cos I'm feeling very faint.*

It went nowhere, and the band felt the production was at fault. '"Apples and Oranges" was destroyed by the production,' said Roger Waters. 'It's a fucking good song.'

Nick Mason explained: 'We had to hustle a bit. It was commercial but we could only do it in two sessions. We prefer to take a longer time.' In many ways, it was their most adventurous single yet, the fuzz guitar reminiscent of the Beatles' 'Sgt Pepper's Lonely Hearts Club Band' (they had been making the 'Pepper' album at Abbey Road at the same time as Floyd were working on 'Piper at the Gates of Dawn'), a similarity which the suddenly shouted words 'We thought you might like to know' makes clear, was far from being a coincidence.

But it certainly needed a George Martin – or a Joe Boyd – to get it right, someone with enough sympathetic toughness, for instance, to ensure that the band actually played in tune, which they didn't, especially in the vital opening seconds, which are a real mess.

Among the never-to-be-released material considered for number three were such titles as 'Scream Thy Last Scream Old Woman With a Casket' (not 'basket', as Pete Frame has it) and 'Vegetable Man', not a farewell nod at Syd (who co-wrote it), but a mordantly savage look at contemporary male mores, a sort of 'Dedicated Follower of Fashion' with teeth: *In yellow shoes I get the blues/So I walk the street with my plastic feet/With blue velvet trousers make me feel pink/There's a kind of stink about/Blue velvet trousers. In my Paisley shirt I look a jerk/And my turquoise waistcoat is quite outasight/But oh – oh my haircut looks so rare . . . So I cover them up with the latest cut . . . And all the lot is what I've got/It's what I wear/It's what you-see/It must be me/It's what I am:/ Vegetable Man . . .*

There's a sort of echo of Frank Zappa's 'Call any Vegetable', or rather *plastic people, you're such a drag* (Zappa had just paid a visit to swingin' London, been snapped on the loo for the famous cover of IT, and found the whole scene wanting, UFO included – or especially).

The disenchantment so evident in 'Vegetable Man' was actually expressed rather better in Rick Wright's B-side to their next single, of which more anon.

'Scream Thy Last Scream' was the first overt expression of the barely suppressed violence which was to come to the fore over later titles, like 'Careful With That Axe, Eugene', 'One of These Days (I'm Going to Cut You Up into Little Pieces)' and the undercurrent of aggro running right through 'Dark Side of the Moon'.

Both 'Scream' and 'Veg' were played on John Peel's Radio 1 'Top Gear' show (the source of the bootleg versions so widely available) and while they are interesting historically for such effects as their use of deliberately excessive echo and making lyrics virtually indecipherable, they weren't really singles.

But then neither were the two tunes eventually chosen.

Peter Jenner, then still their manager, wanted them to make 'Jug Band Blues' (from the forthcoming second album, 'Saucerful of Secrets') the next single, but (in Britain, at least) from now on they were to keep single A-sides and albums rigidly separate until 'The Final Cut' and the poor 'Not Now John' (an appropriate injunction): though 'Careful With That Axe' was issued as a B-side in December 1968, over a year before it was heard on 'Umma Gumma'. But the album version was a live, completely different recording.

'Paint Box' works better, musically, though again the lyric is somewhat inconsequential: *Not that I've had too much to drink/Sitting in a club with so many fools/Playing to rules, trying to impress but feeling rather empty.* Sounds like a reaction to their early outside-London gigs!

Apart from Mason's drumming, it sounds very little like the Floyd today.

'It Would Be So Nice' (Wright)
'Julia Dream' (Waters)
Prod Norman Smith, rec EMI, Abbey Road, Feb 13 1968, rel April 12, 1968

Perhaps because of the hassle of Syd's departure and replacement by Dave Gilmour, which also meant Peter Jenner and Andrew King gave up managing them, their fourth single, with an A-side by Rick Wright and a B-side by Roger Waters, was a complete non-event.

The A-side seems to have vanished without a trace. It wasn't included in the 1971 compilation, 'Relics', a distinction it shares with their next A-side, 'Point Me at the Sky', which was to be their last for 11 years, though Roger Waters says he still likes the song.

Nick Mason's view of 'It Would Be So Nice' is unequivocal: 'Fucking awful, that record, wasn't it? Singles are a funny scene. Some people are prepared to be persuaded into anything. I suppose it all depends on if you want to be a mammoth star or not.'

Remarkable that they should submit to the same syndrome 15 years later, with 'Not Now John'!

'I don't like "It Would Be So Nice",' says Waters. 'I don't like the song or the way it's sung.'

Perhaps it was the superficial similarity of the title to the Beach Boys' 'Wouldn't It Be Nice?' which held it back, but the story the Floyd tells is much more mundane than Brian Wilson's romantic vision of future wedded bliss, as different as Andy Capp compared with Dagwood Bumstead: *Everybody wakes and in the morning/Hot tea, can't stop yawning/Pass the butter please.*

What it sounded more like was another Beatles' out-take, a song trying for the sort of common touch that had made 'Good Morning Good Morning' so appealing, with similar 'Ah-aahh' choruses, but it didn't work.

Again, the BBC was proving difficult, this time over its pet shibboleth: advertising. A line *Have you ever read the Evening Standard?* was objected to, and the band spent £750 to change it to the non-existent Daily Standard (amusingly, in the official lyric book, it becomes *Have you ever read the daily scandal?*, which doesn't even rhyme).

They got some publicity in the Standard for the 'ban', but it didn't make any difference: 'Nobody ever heard it, because it was such a lousy record.' With 'Julia Dream', we begin with a sunny morning bedroom idyll, though the folksy sound was belied by the bleakness under the surface of some of the lyrics which might almost have been penned by Syd. Perhaps that was the idea: *Ev'ry night I turn the light out waiting for the velvet glove/Then that scaly armadillo finds me where I'm hiding . . . /*

Will the misty monster break me? Will the key unlock the door? Will the following footsteps catch me?/Am I really dying?

Julia's dream, dreamboat queen (Again, the lyric book has *dreamboat clean*, which doesn't mean anything.) *Queen upon my dream . . .*

'Point Me at the Sky' (Waters)
'Careful With That Axe, Eugene' (Waters, Wright, Mason, Gilmour)
Prod Norman Smith, rec EMI, Abbey Road, Nov 4 1968, rel Dec 17 1968

'Point Me At the Sky' shows more Beatles influence, this time by 'When I'm 64' with overtones of Tom Lehrer's 'Rickatee-Tickatee-Tin': *If you survive 'til two thousand and five I hope you're exceedingly thin/For if you are stout you will have to breathe out/While the people around you breathe in, breathe in . . .*

But in reality, it's a song of escape from the pressures that were crowding round the Floyd in real life: *Playing the game we know ends in tears/The game we've been playing for thousands and thousands and thousands/Jumps into his cosmic flyer, pulls his plastic collar higher/Light the fuse and stand well back, he cried, this is my last goodbye . . .*

It was another science fiction metaphor, in the tradition begun with Barrett's 'Astronomy Domine' on the first album, not really about space travel as such (any more than 'The Dark Side of the Moon' is about lunar exploration), but utilising the space metaphor to look at the present day, as indeed does the best science fiction.

The B-side, 'Careful With That Axe, Eugene' was the first true Floyd classic, a great instrumental, which surfaced in a live version on the 'Umma Gumma' double album, and then returned, transformed into 'Come In 51, Your Time Is Up', for the explosive climax of 'Zabriskie Point', and a percussive bass line echoed many years later by 'On the Run' on 'Dark Side'.

They were still featuring the tune five years later, at the epochal Earls Court gigs of May 1973 – a long life for a Floyd tune.

Of course, it wasn't really singles material, too good to be a B-side, but without that essential 'hook' to make it as an A-side.

'Embryo' (Waters)
Unauthorised release on EMI Harvest compilation, 'Picnic'
Rel June 1970

Not, strictly speaking, a single, 'Embryo' is one that got away, a song that was included on a 1970 compilation of acts from Harvest, EMI's underground label – to the fury of the group who were on holiday at the time, and said it wasn't ready for release.

That may be so, and compared with the way they were doing the song the next month at the famous Hyde Park open-air concert, Dave Gilmour's contribution was very low-key. However, if it hadn't been for the goof of Malcolm Jones, then the Harvest label manager, and for the nameless benefactors of the rock scene (and for writers like me!) who produce bootlegs, we would have missed a rather beautiful song, one which deserves to stand next to Roger Waters' documentation of the horrors of childhood and adolescence as the unspoilt hope of the unborn.

The lyrics are simple, deceptively so: *All this love is all I am/A ball is all I am/I'm so new compared with you/And I am very small . . . Warm glow, moon glow/Always need a little more room/Whisper low, here I go/I will see the sunshine show.*

The tune is based on a simple but effective bass run, and even on the unfinished version, Rick Wright makes good use of its modal implications in his solo playing. On the live bootleg – or at least on the one I've heard – there is some superb Gilmour guitar.

Explained Dave Gilmour: '"Embryo" was a track that we recorded in about '68 or '69 and we never finished. We all went off it for some reason. We never actually finished the recording of it. It was in a show that we did, called 'The Man and the Journey' or something, originally, and at one point there was talk of doing an album of this show, but we never did it, largely because lots of the material was pinched from other bits we'd already done.

'That was one song that we did but never finished, and EMI got Norman Smith I think to mix it, and they released it without our OK, and that's one of the very very few tracks that we never actually finished. I really don't think there was anything that we actually ever recorded in any form of completion that didn't get released.

'There isn't really a wealth of unreleased material. If we all got killed in a plane crash and they wanted to delve through the archives in order to release 34 other Pink Floyd things they'd have a very hard time.'

'Embryo' is one from the vaults they should definitely issue in an official version some day.

'Another Brick in the Wall, Part Two' (Waters)
'One of My Turns' (Waters)
Rel November 16 1979

Not surprisingly, they concentrated (in UK, at least), for the next 11 years on albums, until in November 1979, 'Another Brick in the Wall, Part Two' was to give them their most successful single, selling over a million copies in the UK alone in only two months.

So much had happened between the two that some might argue that the Floyd of 'Careful With That Axe' and 'Another Brick in the Wall' are two entirely different bands, even though the personnel on both was the same.

In many ways it was an ironic commentary upon the band's isolation from the political realities of life in Thatcher's England, that a left-wing socialist like Roger Waters should get a group of comprehensive schoolkids to sing 'we don't need no education' at a time of savage Government cuts in educational expenditure.

On the other hand, the song struck a responsive chord among black kids striking against educational apartheid in Soweto, and was promptly banned by the South African regime.

What was really remarkable was that, having been written off for years by the hip music writers as creators of middle class muzak, they could suddenly touch a contemporary nerve with a single that owed nothing to the Floyd's past track record, and which was bought by many who probably thought they were a new group. Not only that, but, as the film of 'The Wall' makes obvious with its Gerald Scarfe cartoons of mortar-boarded teachers wielding canes, it's clearly not a comprehensive school Roger Waters had in mind. For whatever reason, the caricature worked – perhaps because it appealed to the same collective subconscious which responds to images of mortar-boarded teachers wielding canes (now banned in most British schools) in the Beano and Dandy comics – giving the band an unexpected success that they couldn't repeat with the 12in single from 'The Final Cut', featuring a remixed version of 'Not Now John'.

'Not Now John'/'The Hero's Return' (parts I and II/ 'Not Now John' (album version)

In a sense, 'The Final Cut' is a reversion to the Floyd as an album band, and it seems likely that the single was released only at the insistence of the record company in the hope of another platinum disc. And while 'Not Now John' was obviously the strongest choice, it didn't have the black-and-white, hard-edged simplicity of the 1979 success, even when remixed.

Gilmour is quite frank about his dislike of 'Not Now John' as a single. 'I don't like that at all,' he says. And he agrees that its release was the result of record company pressure for 'the single from the album'.

'They always say it makes a vast difference to record sales if you have a single, even if it doesn't sell any, that just because of the bit of airplay you get on AM radio in America it makes a lot of difference to your album sales. Of course, nobody knows if it makes any difference or not but it's the standard record company ploy that they use, and a managerial ploy as well. 'We more or less fell for a record company hype, when they talked about it. We did discuss all the tracks on it to see if there was a good record. I said I didn't think there was. Steve (O'Rourke, their manager) said that in America all the radio stations wanted 'Not Now John' out as a single, and I think we just went along with it.'

There were obvious problems with making a hit out of a song whose first word was the forbidden Mother Goddess invocation, 'fuck', and when promo copies were first sent to America DJs they were of an 'obscured' version, on which the dread four-letters had been changed to the five-letter euphemism, 'stuff'.

This was the version which became the single, though the B-side of the 12in 45 had the full, unexpurgated words.

'The fact is,' Gilmour points out, 'it still says "fuck all that" afterwards because it's just a copy of the master, with me in the studio and some backing singers in the studio shouting "stuff!" a bit louder than "fuck".'

The song is actually ambiguous, a reaction by part of Roger Waters to the main subject of the album, which is the betrayal of the postwar dream, ending up in a description of a nightmare that would be ludicrous if it weren't so tragic; a tinpot Boadicea rattling her gunboats in the South Atlantic, risking the atomic debacle of the album's last song.

'Fuck all that!' says the song, in those very words, so let's get the show on the road, and have a good time: *Not nah John/We've got to get on with the film show/Hollywood waits at the end of the rainbow/Who cares what it's about/As long as the kids go?/Not now John/Got to get on with the show.*

The reference to Hollywood makes one think its inspiration might almost have been one of the many battles behind the making of the 'Wall' movie. But though one imagines the song being sung by Alan Parker, or even Dave Gilmour, who probably shares Waters' opinion of the Falklands adventure even if he has strong reservations about the album, or perhaps a roadie, Roger Waters says it is his *own* voice.

'It's a very schizophrenic song, because there's this one character singing the verses who's become irritated by all this whining and moaning about how desperate things are, the Falklands and so on, and doesn't want to hear any of it any more, and there's part of me in that.

'Then there's this other voice which keeps harping back to earlier songs, saying *make them laugh, make them cry, make them dance in the aisles*, which is from "Teach"' (actually called 'One of the Few' on the album). 'So it's a strange song.

'But what the first voice is saying is very straightforward: *Fuck all that, we've got to get on with these*: there's no time to think about any of that, we've got to learn how to make these things quicker than the Japanese can, which is ludicrous of course, there's no way we can compete with the Japanese.

'Now, that's something that I think we should be proud of, the fact that we can't become part of the machine successfully.

'It makes life a bit uncomfortable, if we're living a life where the ethic is to compete with everybody else and sell more goods to the Third World or each other or whoever it might be, you know, to win that particular race. So it makes it difficult, but it's something, it's a difficulty I'd rather be coping with than living in Japan.

'Mind you, this is easy for me to say. I'm not on the dole!'

More interesting, to the Floyd completist, is the fact that the 12in single has a previously unreleased final verse and chorus for 'The Hero's Return' (it's hardly significant enough to be described as 'part II', as the label has it) which underpins the post-war relevance of the hero's experiences over fire-bombed Dresden. This is 'Slaughterhouse 5' from the air, a war in which the killers are just as much victims as the killed.

To promote the single, Waters put together a video promo which was also released by Picture Music as a 'video EP'.

It is interesting to view this in the light of Waters' dissatisfaction with Alan Parker's work on 'The Wall' movie, because in an age when some of the most exciting visual effects are being obtained in pop video promos – (albeit with scant regard for the songs' lyrical content, if any) the 'Not Now John' promo is really not very good.

Parker is never boring, but there are long stretches of this four-part distillation of 'The Final Cut', especially the promo for the single, 'Not Now John', which really drag. The four items are given a spurious unity by all being viewed by Alex McAvoy (who played the teacher in 'The Wall') on a family TV set, intercut with shots from the Falklands War.

The video credit says 'screenplay by Roger Waters, produced by Barry Matthews, directed by Willie Christie' and later Roger was to accept responsibility for the basic idea, but not the execution.

'The conceptions on paper, some of them,' he told me, 'the man losing his son and going off to wreak his revenge on Margaret Thatcher was mine. Apart from that it's nothing to do with me, really.

'I wanted to spend all the money that was available on a Sam Peckinpah scene, with blood everywhere, really expensive special effects, but they're so expensive that if you do that there's nothing left.'

The really sad thing about this missed opportunity is that, there are glimpses of the powerfully moving production this could have been. It could have worked as an antidote to the 'Gotcha!' jingoism of the Sun and the rest of the press.

The Lyrics

> *Strangers passing in the street*
> *By chance two separate glances meet.*
> *And I am you and what you see is me.*
> *And do I take you by the hand*
> *And lead you through the land*
> *And help me understand the best I can?*
>
> – 'Echoes'

When Orson Welles, playing Clarence Darrow the great radical lawyer in the film of Ira Levin's 'Compulsion', was criticized for defending two rich kids on trial for committing a completely pointless murder, he said he thought the rich had every right to the same standards of defence as the poor. And since rock stars are human, too, it's unlikely that their problems of identity will be very different from yours and mine.

In fact, since they are more in the grip of the money market than most ordinary wage slaves, they may illuminate the same problems more dramatically for us, especially if they have the inner vision and expressive ability to generalize from their particular experience.

In an alienated world, one of the most alienating ideas is that it is anti-social to be concerned with inner reality. Is any sort of social progress possible if members of society do not learn to handle their individual hang-ups?

The individual/society disjunction is a special application of the mind/body dichotomy which has plagued Western philosophy since Pythagoras: the 'real' world is all we can touch, including our own arms and legs and faces and genitals, and the religious and the materialists are united in denying any interaction between what happens 'outside us' and what happens 'inside'.

In the lyrics of Roger Waters – and I think that everyone, including his co-members past and present, will agree that his are the most significant lyrics in the works of Pink Floyd – the concern with the torments of the soul is set against two very *real* outer realities: the death of his father in the war, and the contradictory position of the rock megastar, whose every attempt to communicate with his huge audience is sabotaged by its very size.

The concern with war heroes as victims can be traced back to the half-serious, half-jokey story of Corporal Clegg on the second album:

> *Corporal Clegg, umbrella in the rain,*
> *He's never been the same,*
> *No one is to blame.*
> *Corporal Clegg received his medal in a dream*
> *From Her Majesty the Queen.*
> *His boots were very clean.*
>
> *Mrs Clegg you must be proud of him,*
> *Mrs Clegg another drop of gin.'*

The image of widows waiting in the rain was echoed 15 years later by the picture of women waving their men away to sail to the Falklands:

> *They disembarked in 45*
> *and no one spoke and no one smiled*
> *there were too many spaces in the line*
> *gathered at the Cenotaph*
> *all agreed with hand on heart*
> *to sheath the sacrificial knives*
>
> *but now*
>
> *She stands upon Southampton Dock*
> *with her handkerchief*
> *and her summer frock clings*
> *to her wet body in the rain*
> *in quiet desperation knuckles*
> *white upon the slippery reins*
> *she bravely waves the boys goodbye again.*
> — 'Southampton Dock' ('The Final Cut')

The reference to his own dead father was first made specific in the song, 'Free Four', written in 1969 for the soundtrack of Barbet Schroeder's film, 'La Vallee', released in the English-speaking world as 'Obscured By Clouds' (also the title of Floyd's soundtrack album). The Floyd had previously composed the music for Schroeder's rather exploitative film about swinging Paris, 'More', for which they were paid £600 each, good money in those days for a week's work. Schroeder is an ex-film critic (for Les Cahiers du Cinema) and associate of Jean Luc-Godard whose most notable achievement was to produce Eric Rohmer's superb 'Ma Nuit Chez Maud' in 1969. He had also shot a documentary in New Guinea, which was the setting for 'La Vallee', a fairly typical piece for its time about rich hippies going native in the jungle. But Waters introduced a note of stark realism to a surprisingly jaunty tune:

> You are the angel of death
> And I am the dead man's son.
>
> He was buried like a mole in a foxhole
> And everyone's still on the run.
>
> But who is the master of foxhounds,
> And who says the hunt has begun,
>
> And who calls the tune in the courtroom
> And who beats the funeral drum?

Eric Fletcher Waters was killed in the battle for the Anzio bridgehead in early 1944, a blundered attempt to cut off von Runstedt's Nazi armies in the battle for Italy by landing behind their fortified Gustav line. The British forces were pinned down for five months in a debacle comparable to the one fought for the Gallipoli bridgehead in World War I. 40,000 British soldiers died against a toll of 20,000 enemy troops, although it was the Germans who were caught by surprise.

That was the time Lady Astor made a speech suggesting that the Eighth Army were lucky because they'd dodged D-Day. The soldiers wore the 'D-Day Dodger' tag with as much pride as, earlier, they'd accepted Field-Marshal Rommel's description of them as 'desert rats', and composed a little ditty to the soldier's tune on both sides, 'Lilli Marlene', in the honourable lady's honour:

> We're the D-Day Dodgers out in Italy
> Always on the vino, always on the spree.
> Eighth Army scroungers and their tanks
> We live in Rome among the Yanks.
> We are the D-Day Dodgers in sunny Italy.
>
> We landed at Salerno, a holiday with pay,
> The Gerries brought the bands out to greet us on our way,
> Showed us the sights and made us tea,
> We all sang songs, the beer was free,
> To welcome D-Day Dodgers to sunny Italy.
>
> Naples and Cassino were taken in our stride
> We didn't go to fight there, we just went for the ride.
> Anzio and Sangro were just names,
> We only went to look for dames,
> The artful D-Day Dodgers in sunny Italy . . .

Dear Lady Astor, you think you know a lot,
Standing on your platform and talking tommy-rot.
You're England's sweetheart and her pride,
We think yer mouth's too bleeding wide,
That's from the D-Day Dodgers in sunny Italy.

Look around the mountains in the mud and rain,
You'll find the scattered crosses, some that have no name.
Heart-ache and pain and suffering gone,
The boys beneath them slumber on;
Those are the D-Day Dodgers who'll stay in Italy.

It was the likes of Lady Astor (not all of them on the Tory benches) who were responsible for the betrayal of the 'post-war dream' for which 'The Final Cut' was composed as a requiem.

The story of his father's death was told most explicitly in the song he wrote for the 'Wall' movie, 'When the Tigers Broke Free' (the Tiger was the Wehrmacht Panzer Divisions' most potent tank in World War II):

It was just before dawn
One miserable morning in black '44
When the Forward Commander was
asked to sit tight, when he asked
That his men be withdrawn.
The general gave thanks
as the other ranks held back
the enemy tanks for a while.

And kind old King George
Sent Mother a note
When he heard that Father was gone
It was I recall in the form of a scroll
with gold leaf and all
And I found it one day
in a drawer of old photographs, hidden away.
And my eyes still grow damp to remember
His Majesty signed with his own rubber stamp . . .

It was dark all around
There was frost on the ground
When the Tigers broke free.
And no one survived from
The Royal Fusiliers Company C
They were all left behind

> *Most of them dead*
> *The rest of them dying*
> *And that's how the High Command*
> *Took my Daddy from me*

The song is a valuable addition to 'The Wall', putting the story in perspective and rooting the childlike bewilderment of 'Another Brick in the Wall, Part I' in concrete reality:

> *Daddy's flown across the sea*
> *Leaving just a memory*
> *A snap shot in the family album*
> *Daddy what else did you leave for me*
> *All in all it was just a brick in the wall . . .*

It was originally intended to include 'Tigers' on 'The Final Cut' (when it was planned as a 'Wall' soundtrack album), and in fact when the album was halfway finished, Roger rang me up and played me a remixed, edited version over the 'phone. It's a pity he changed his mind, because it's an important element in the Eric Fletcher story.

The song can be heard, however, on the video of the movie.

In 'Dark Side of the Moon', he describes war as a chessgame, with the generals far behind the lines in their bunkers:

> *Forward he cried from the rear*
> *and the front rank died*
> *And the general sat, and the lines on the map*
> *moved from side to side*
> *Black and blue*
> *And who knows which is which and who is who*
> *Up and Down*
> *And in the end it's only round and round and round*
> *Haven't you heard it's a battle of words*
> *the poster bearer cried*
> *Listen son, said the man with the gun*
> *There's room for you inside.*

Us and Them

Much more is made of the military causes of the hang-ups of young Pink in the 'Wall' movie than in the album or live concerts, including a very powerful opening montage sequence cross-cutting between a crowd rushing into a concert arena and soldiers going over the top. But all the references to war in his earlier work lead to 'The Final Cut', the Floyd's last (and possibly final) album.

It is heralded somewhat by the snatch of lyric about Vera Lynn towards the end of 'The Wall', which leads into the 'Bring the boys back home' sequence. (Roger is too young to remember, but the slow demobilization after the war made it a potent slogan equal to the earlier 'Second Front Now'. Soldiers and airmen overseas went on strike in a frightening prelude to what was to happen in the 1945 General Election. One ex-squaddie told me: 'We were ready to have Joe for king and Pollitt for pope.' Joe, of course, was Stalin, and Pollitt was Harry Pollitt, general secretary of the Communist Party of Great Britain.)

The Falklands brought the reality of war home to us in a way that Korea, and the death throes of colonialism in Kenya, Malaya, Cyprus, Aden and Ireland had failed to do. Anyone who sat, glued to the TV set in 1982, watching the Falklands task force sail halfway across the world to protect a barren outcropping of rock from the Antarctic landmass from being reclaimed by the Argentinians, and watched as troops were ferried ashore from the blazing wrecks, must feel a shudder of remembered horror at the very titles of the songs, ringing like names on a casualty list: 'The Post-War dream . . .' 'Your Possible Pasts' . . . 'One of the Few' . . . 'The Hero's Return' . . . 'The Gunner's Dream' . . . 'Paranoid Eyes' . . . 'Get Your Filthy Hands Off My Desert' . . . 'The Fletcher Memorial Home' . . . 'Southampton Dock' . . . 'The Final Cut' . . .

As the recurrent chorus of 'The Final Cut' demands to know:

> *Oh Maggie, Maggie what have we done?*

The end of 'Southampton Dock' reveals that the title of the album has a wider significance than the history of a rock and roll band:

> *and still the dark stain spreads between*
> *his shoulder blades*
> *a mute reminder of the poppy fields and graves*
> *and when the fight was over*
> *we spent what they had made*
> *but in the bottom of our hearts*
> *we felt the final cut.*

A sub-plot through the earlier songs tells the story of an ex-serviceman turning to teaching as a means of making ends meet, *trying to clout these little ingrates into shape*, drinking to roll away reality:

> *now you're lost in a haze of alcohol soft middle age*
> *the pie in the sky turned out to be miles too high*
> *you hide hide hide*
> *behind brown and mild eyes.*   – Paranoid Eyes

The sympathy of this portrait has to be set against the caricature of the school-teacher in 'The Wall', and is a good illustration of the way Waters links together the exterior worlds with interior agony, no better epitomised than in the title song, which zooms in from the wide canvas of the rest of the album to focus on the insecurities of (presumably) the writer:

> and if I show you my dark side
> will you still hold me tonight
> and if I open my heart to you
> and show you my weak side
> what would you do?
> would you sell your story to Rolling Stone?
> Would you take the children away
> and leave me alone
> and smile in reassurance
> as you whisper down the phone
> would you send me packing
> or would you take me home?
>
> thought I oughta bare my naked feelings
> thought I oughta tear the curtain down
> I held the blade in trembling hands
> prepared to make it but just then the 'phone rang
> I had never had the nerve to make the final cut.
>
> – The Final Cut

It's always dangerous to seek autobiographical clues in a writer's work. Some, like James Joyce or Marcel Proust, will detail the mundane and mystical experiences of a lifetime so that the reader can taste the very flavour of a petit Madeleine cake, or smell the perfume between Molly Bloom's thighs. For others, experience is just the raw material, the paint on the palette before the brush mixes it into living colour. When I tackled him about how close he was to Pink in 'The Wall', he ticked off the similarities and differences for me:

'My father was killed in the war, at Anzio. I did find the scroll and the uniform in a drawer one day.

'No hotel-room smashing up, no mad shaving of anything, that is a bit of Syd, definitely. Did get divorced, trouble with the old lady at home, but I never turned into a pink blob.'

The character of Syd Barrett, and the subject of madness, looms large over Floyd's work, as might be expected.

Before they'd started work on 'Dark Side of the Moon' proper, Roger had already written the song, 'Brain Damage', with the lunatic who is *on the grass* at the beginning, *in my head* at the end: *there's someone in my head but it's not me*, concluding:

> *And if the band you're in starts playing different tunes*
> *I'll see you on the dark side of the moon.*

Before that, madness had lurked in the very titles of many of the band's earlier songs, like 'One of These Days I'm Going to Chop You Up Into Little Pieces', abbreviated – for safety's sake? – to just 'One of These Days' on the sleeve and label of 'Meddle'.

And on the same album, 'Fearless' counterposed the behaviour of a fool climbing a hill (sounds familiar?) with the exultant singing of a football crowd:

> *Fearlessly the idiot faced the crowd,*
> *Smiling,*
> *Merciless the magistrate turns round,*
> *Frowning,*
> *And who's the fool who wears the crown*
> *Go down in your own way*
> *And every day is the right day*
> *And as you rise above the fear lines in his brow*
> *You look down and hear the sound of the faces in the crowd.*

Syd came to full stage centre, however, in 'Wish You Were Here', though it's dangerous to see it only as an album about him. It's about alienation, lack of communication and, as Roger has pointed out, it's about the band themselves, who were barely talking to each other at that point.

'The album was very difficult,' recalled Roger later. 'It was a bloody difficult thing to do, and it didn't quite come off, but it nearly happened. The basic track was terribly fucking hard to do because we were all out of it and you can hear it. I can always hear it: kind of mechanical and heavy.

'That's why I'm so glad people are copping the sadness of it – that in spite of ourselves, we did manage to get something down, we did manage to get somewhat of what was going on in those sessions down on vinyl. 'By the time we were finishing it, after the second American tour, I hadn't got an ounce of creative energy left in me anywhere, and those last couple of weeks were a real fucking struggle.'

Remembering the hard feelings that accompanied Syd's departure from the group, and the change in management that ensued, the song 'Shine On You Crazy Diamond' must be one of the most remarkable tributes to an ex-member ever to be put out by a band:

Remember when you were young, you shone like the sun
    Shine on you crazy diamond
Now there's a look in your eyes like black holes in the sky
    Shine on you crazy diamond
You were caught on the crossfire of childhood and stardom,
    blown on the steel breeze,
Come on you target for faraway laughter,
come on you stranger, you legend, you martyr, and shine . . .

Come on you raver, you seer of visions,
come on you painter, you piper, you prisoner, and shine . . .

Come on you boy child, you winner and loser,
come on you miner for truth and delusion, and shine.
    – Shine On You Crazy Diamond (Wish You Were Here)

The song drew its inspiration, said Roger, from the loud four-note guitar phrase from Dave Gilmour which opens the album. 'I don't know why I started writing those lyrics about Syd. I think it was because that phrase of Dave's was an extremely kind of mournful sound.

I'm very sad about Syd. I wasn't for years. For years I suppose he was a threat because of all that bollocks written about him and us. Of course he was very important and the band would never have fucking started without him because he was writing all the material. It couldn't have happened without him but on the other hand it couldn't have gone on *with* him.

'But when he came to the 'Wish You Were Here' sessions – ironic in itself – to see this great fat, bald, mad person . . . the first day he came, I was in fucking tears.

'"Shine On" is not really about Syd. He's just a symbol for all the extremes of absence some people have to indulge in because it's the only way they can cope with how fucking sad it is – modern life, to withdraw completely.'

Consider the inner problems of the rock megastar, who starts out as the first among equals, mirroring the experience of a generation, and ends up as dictator. It's all very well for Bob Dylan to say 'I can't think for you, you've got to decide' and 'don't follow leaders', but that's precisely what he ends up doing, being a leader in spite of himself, and doing the thinking for his followers.

If it wasn't for the fact that he addresses himself to this specific contradiction, Roger Waters' depictions of the hell of life on the road would be no more significant than those of Joni Mitchell, say:

> *Remember the days when you used to sit*
> *And make up your tunes for love*
> *And pour your simple sorrow*
> *To the soundhole and your knee*
> *And now you're seen*
> *On giant screens*
> *And at parties for the press*
> *And for people who have slices of you*
> *From the company*
> *They toss around your latest golden egg*
> *Speculation – well, who's to know*
> *If the next one in the nest*
> *Will glitter for them so . . .*
>
> For the Roses

Not that Roger Waters doesn't also chronicle the sheer heart-breaking banality of much of the rock lifestyle:

> *A butterfly with broken wings is falling by your side*
> *The ravens all are closing in, there's nowhere you can hide.*
> *Your manager and agent are both busy on the phone*
> *Selling coloured photographs to magazines back home.*
>
> – Cymbaline (More)

And anyone who has dealt with the animals – there is no other word, believe me – who control the dollars and cents, the pounds and pence of the music industry, will recognize the accuracy of the words ascribed to the manager-agent:

> *We're just knocked out. We heard about the sell out*
> *   You gotta get an album out.*
> *You owe it to the people. We're so happy we can hardly count.*
> *Everybody else is just green, have you seen the Chart?*
> *It's a helluva start, it could be made into a monster*
> *   if we all pull together as a team.*
> *And if we tell you the name of the game, boy,*
> *   we call it Riding the Gravy Train.*
>
> – Have A Cigar (Wish You Were Here)

The same theme is present among the firecracker rhythms of the song listing the emptiness of a life where everything has its pricetag:

> *Grab that cash with both hands and make a stash*
> *New car, caviar, four-star daydream*
> *Think I'll buy me a football team*
>> *– 'Money' ('Dark Side of the Moon')*

(It's reported that Pink Floyd lost £2½ million when the investment company handling their money, Norton Warburg, crashed in 1981.)

Those familiar with 'The Wall' will recognize those lines as the ones seized upon by the teacher and read out in derision to the class: 'What have we here, laddie? Mysterious scribblings? A secret code? No, poems, no less. Poems, everybody. The laddie reckons himself as a poet . . . Absolute rubbish, laddie! Get on wi'yer wu'rrk! Repeat after me . . .'

Judging by 'The Wall', Roger sees education as part of the conditioning process by which children are taught to respect authority, and to suppress their own feelings, a process carried out by those who are themselves victims of similar repressions in their own lives:

> *When we grew up and went to school*
> *There were certain teachers who would*
> *Hurt the children any way they could*
> *By pouring their derision*
> *Upon anything we did,*
> *And exposing every weakness,*
> *However carefully hidden by the kids*
> *But in the town, it was well known,*
> *When they got home at night, their fat and*
> *Psychopathic wives would thrash them*
> *Within inches of their lives.*
>> *– 'The Happiest Days of Our Lives' ('The Wall')*

So authority is itself rooted in feet of clay. And inasmuch as he sets himself up (or is set up) as an authority figure, there isn't a great deal to choose between the fascist demagogue and the posturing of the rock star. In 'The Wall', Pink starts off haranguing the audience in terms that suggest there is something rather nasty beneath the surface of his performance:

> *So ya*
> *Thought ya*
> *Might like to go to the show.*
> *To feel the warm thrill of confusion,*
> *That space cadet glow.*

> *Tell me is something eluding you sunshine?*
> *Is this not what you expected to see?*
> *If you'd like to find out what's behind these cold eyes*
> *You'll just have to claw your way through this*
> *Disguise . . .*
>
> — 'In the Flesh'

But later, as the skin has been stripped from his hero, the fascism becomes more specific in the reprise of the same song:

> *. . . we're going to find out where you fans*
> *Really stand.*
> *Are there any queers in the audience tonight?*
> *Get 'em up against the wall.*
> *There's one in the spotlight,*
> *He don't look right to me,*
> *Get him up against the wall.*
> *That one looks Jewish,*
> *And that one's a coon.*
> *Who let this riff raff into the room?*
> *There's one smoking a joint and*
> *Another with spots,*
> *If I had my way*
> *I'd have you all shot.*

Ten years or so before Roger Waters was born, when Sir Oswald Mosley's British Union of Fascists was having a last fling before World War II destroyed its mass support, this was precisely the technique that was used to isolate hecklers or outsiders at the mass rallies at places like Olympia and Earls Court – ironically, the latter the very hall where 'The Wall' was performed in London: a spotlight would isolate intruders, stewards would converge from all corners of the hall, and Mosley would resume speaking only when the outsiders were carried out, beaten and bleeding, and flung into the waiting arms of the police (who not infrequently arrested them for breaches of the peace).

In my book, 'Singers of an Empty Day', I examined the role of the superstar as demagogue in some details, and I quoted the great (and martyred) post-Freudian psychologist, Wilhelm Reich on why the troubled German worker (17 million citizens of the Weimar Republic voted National Socialist out of a total of 33 million voters) voluntarily surrendered to Hitler and his fellow gangsters the responsibility for coping with the hazards of the world around him.

'Passing this responsibility enthusiastically from himself to some

Fuehrer or politician has become one of his essential characteristics,' wrote Reich, 'since he is no longer able to understand either himself or his institutions, of which he is only afraid. Fundamentally, he is helpless, incapable of freedom, and craving for authority, for he cannot react spontaneously; he is armoured and expects commands, for he is full of contradictions and cannot rely upon himself.' ('The Function of the Orgasm')

Interestingly, though he says the only psychological writing he is at all familiar with is Jung (and that only slightly), Reich's concept of 'armour' as a pathological symptom is remarkably close to Roger Waters' 'Wall'.

Reich: 'Patients complain of "being tense to the point of bursting", "filled to the point of exploding". They feel themselves "blown up". They fear any attack upon their armouring because it makes them feel as if they were being "pricked open". Some patients said that they were afraid of "dissolving" or "melting", of losing their "grip on themselves", or their "contour". They clung to the rigid armourings of their movements and attitudes like a drowning man to a ship's planks. The most cherished wish of others was "to burst" . . .

'The neurotic patient has developed a "stiff" body periphery, while retaining a lively inner core. He feels "uncomfortable within his own skin", "inhibited", unable to "realise himself", as if he "were immured", "without contact", "tense to the point of bursting". He strives with all available means "toward the world", but it is as if he "were tied down". More than that, his efforts to come into contact with life are often so painful, he is so ill-equipped to endure the difficulties and disappointments of life, that he prefers "to crawl into himself". Thus, the direction of the biological function "toward the world", "from the inside toward the outside", is counteracted by a "moving away form the world", a "withdrawal into self".'

Waters: *There is no pain, you are receding,*
A distant ship smoke on the horizon,
You are only coming through in waves,
Your lips move but I can't hear what you're saying.
When I was a child I had a fever,
My hands felt just like two balloons.
Now, I've got that feeling once again,
I can't explain, you would not understand,
This is not how I am,
I have become
Comfortably numb.

OK
Just a little pin prick,
There'll be no more aaaaaah!
But you may feel a little sick.
Can you stand up?
I do believe it's working. Good.
That'll keep you going through the show.
Come on it's time to go . . .

      – 'Comfortably Numb'

Hey you! with your ear against the wall
Waiting for someone to call, would you touch me?
Hey you! Would you help me to carry the stone?
Open your heart, I'm coming home.
But it was only fantasy.
The wall was too high, as you can see.
No matter how he tried he could not break free.
And the worms ate into his brain.
Hey you! out there on the road
Just doing what you're told, can you help me?
Hey you! out there beyond the wall
Breaking bottles in the hall, can you help me?
Hey you! don't tell me there's no hope at all,
Together we stand, divided we fall.

      – 'Hey You'

Crazy, over the rainbow, I am crazy,
Bars in the window,
There must have been a door there in the wall
When I came in.
Crazy, over the rainbow, he is crazy.
The evidence before the court is
Incontrovertible, there's no need for
the jury to retire . . .
But my friend, you have revealed your
Deepest fear.
I sentence you to be exposed before
Your peers
Tear down the wall.

      – 'The Trial'

The remarkable thing about 'The Wall', is that while it may be 'the downer of all time' (guitarist Andy Roberts, who played in the surrogate band), it ends on an incredibly 'up' note.

But this is true, also, of 'Dark Side of the Moon', with the wonderful litany of 'Eclipse' at the end, of 'Wish You Were Here', with the almost exultant final chorus of the reprise of 'Shine On Your Crazy Diamond', and, to bring things up to date, the conclusion of Roger Waters' first solo album, 'The Pro's and Cons of Hitch-Hiking'.

Here, inner and outer reality come directly into conflict, for the entire sequence is a nightmare, where images from the 'real' world become symbols for the hero's own conflicts, his fears, desires, ambitions, and his sexual fantasies.

It is, perhaps, revealing how predatory are the women in Roger Waters' lyrics. It's so long since we've had anything as lyrically erotic as the symbolism in 'Echoes':

> *Cloudless every day you fall*
> *Upon my waking eyes.*
> *Inviting and inciting me to rise,*
> *And through the window in the wall*
> *Come streaming in on sunlight wings*
> *A million bright-ambassadors of morning.*
>
> *And no one sings me lullabies*
> *And no one makes me close my eyes*
> *And so I throw the windows wide*
> *And call to you across the sky.*

Later, Waters' heroes are all victimised by women: by the mother and the wife in 'The Wall' (are they the same character?), and by the various women in 'Pros and Cons'. But, he points out, the concluding note of that album is positive:

'Certainly, it's partly about bad relationships with women,' he agreed. 'It's also about good relationships with women. That is the point of the whole thing, and how it finishes up is how I've finished up, now. Feeling good. But in the past I've had bad times. I mean, however good a relationship is, it's bound to feel bad some of the time, unless you're very comfortably numb, or very numbly comfortable.

'Some of my relationships have been bad in the past, yes. Certainly 'The Wall' was about that. It was drawn largely from my relationship with my first wife, I suppose, and the divorce and all the rest of it. And some of this is, too.'

Seen in this way, it is hard to cut 'Pro's and Cons' off from the rest of the work, and it's hardly surprising. The guitarist at his concerts may be Eric rather than Dave, but Roger is still Roger.

The Albums

The Piper at the Gates of Dawn
Prod Norman Smith, rec EMI, Abbey Road, April 1967, rel Aug 5 1967

> Astronomy Domine (Barrett)
> Lucifer Sam (Barrett)
> Matilda Mother (Barrett)
> Flaming (Barrett)
> Pow R. Toc H. (Barrett, Waters, Wright, Mason)
> Take Up Thy Stethoscope and Walk (Waters)
>
> Interstellar Overdrive (Barrett, Waters, Wright, Mason)
> The Gnome (Barrett)
> Chapter 24 (Barrett)
> The Scarecrow (Barrett)
> Bike (Barrett)

> *Lest the awe should dwell*
> *And turn your frolic to fret*
> *You shall look on my power at the helping hour*
> *But then you shall forget!*
>
> – Kenneth Grahame

Even now, 18 years after its release, Pink Floyd's first album is an impressive work. In comparison with the two singles they had released by August 1967 – and bearing in mind that five tracks of it were actually recorded *before* 'See Emily Play' – 'The Piper at the Gates of Dawn' displays a remarkable maturity, and one can sense the excitement of a group of creative people seeing just what can be achieved with the four tracks available to them on the tapes at Abbey Road.

Compared with today's 32 tracks and more, of course, four-track recording was fairly limiting, demanding a good deal of 'bouncing' from track to track to get it all down (resulting in a strange feeling of distance, even alienation, created by the build-up of background noise on the tape from so much re-recording, which is particularly noticeable with Phil Spector's famous 'wall of sound' recordings, many of which were recorded on *three*-track). However, more is not better: it's doubtful if anyone has ever used the recording studio as creatively as the Beatles and George Martin did on 'Sgt Pepper', and while 'Piper' is not quite in that class, it was well deserving of the plaudits it received from the Fab Four, who dropped in on them one April afternoon to give it a listen.

> *Music seems to help the pain*
> *Seems to motivate the brain.*
> *Doctor kindly tell your wife that I'm alive*
> *Flowers thrive.*

'Lucifer Sam' is about a Siamese cat, but even here Syd's growing paranoia looms in more word-play lyrics like *I'd like to drown in sifting sands padding around on the ground, duty bound when you're around. That cat's something I can't explain.* The current preoccupations of the underground break through in the lines *Ginger gentle you're a witch/ You're the left side he's the right side . . .* The right hemisphere of the brain (in right-handed people, at least) is believed to be the part related to intuition and artistic endeavour while the left hemisphere is devoted to reasoning, logic and calculation. There was much talk at the time about connecting the two, possibly by surgery, or transferring control from one to the other with drugs. It made a pleasant change from the standard astrological 'what's your star sign?' greeting.

There's an interesting solo on the lower strings of the guitar, which anticipates some of the bass-dominated tunes of later Floyd during the ascendancy of Roger Waters.

Two songs appear at first sight to be concerned with another preoccupation: fairy stories of gnomes and magic kings, epitomised by the undeserved popularity of J. R. R. Tolkien's fantasies upon themes worked much more effectively by Richard Wagner. 'Matilda Mother' however, is more profound, concentrating upon the change of focus in a child's mind when the story book is closed and the light goes out, in which the lyrics have a crystal clarity unusual in such songs:

> *Oh mother, tell me more.*
> *Why'd you have to leave me there, hanging in my infant*
> *air waiting?*
> *You only have to read the lines as scribbly black and*
> *everything shines . . .*

Richard Wright has an interesting 'modal' solo on the basis of a repeated B minor chord which in live performance tended to be much longer.

Wright himself felt that this was the direction in which the band should be going, especially in live performance, where the constraints of the three-minute single were too limiting.

'Things we do live tend to be longer so we have time to develop them,' he said later. 'As a group, we've never been interested in going on stage, doing three minutes, then stopping, and then going on to do another three minutes. The whole tradition has been to go on stage and improvise. In the old days we used to do a hell of a lot of it. Some numbers we'd do for half an hour.'

They were not really to capture this feeling on record until 'Saucerful of Secrets' on their next album.

Apart from its remarkably sophisticated chord sequence, with a surprising modulation on the bridge, 'The Gnome' is a much less distinguished song, sung very straight against an acoustic-sounding guitar and celeste from Wright.

This song, and 'Scarecrow', represented the sort of fey direction flower power was to take with the original Tyrannosaurus Rex and Joe Boyd's other great protégés, (the only successful developers of that rather soppy tradition), Mike Heron and Robin Williamson's Incredible String Band. Both songs have similar moods, though 'Scarecrow' is blacker. After an intro of right-handed organ (played entirely on the black notes in two sharps) from Rick Wright, against a tick-tock rhythm, Barrett's strangely appealing, faux-naif voice intones the non-story of the character who *stood in a field where barley grows*, evoking rather than describing the fenland country to the east of Cambridge, ending on a note of resignation: *The black and green scarecrow was sadder than me* (a revealing comment from the alleged madcap), *now he's resigned to his fate, his life, not unkind, he doesn't mind*. The band only really comes in for the play-out, which ends tantalisingly almost before it's begun. A pity; it's a song that might have benefited from a stronger, more developed treatment. As it is, it's a trifle.

In 'Bike', the influence of the Beatles becomes stronger as the rallantando last verse,

> *I know a room of musical tunes*
> *So write some chief*
> *Most of them have got one*
> *Let's go into the other room and make them work*

leads into a brief musical collage of concrete sounds rather like a Revolution No 8½'.

'Chapter 24' reads like sections from some psychedelic book of the dead, or perhaps an interpretation of an 'I Ching' hexagram (*Change returns success . . . Action brings good fortune*). There is an interesting right-hand modal solo from Rick Wright under and after the final A major chord of the song.

Syd named the album after a chapter of Kenneth Grahame's lovely children's book, 'The Wind in the Willows', describing Mole and Rat's encounter with the Great God Pan:

'. . . and then, in that utter clearness of the imminent dawn, while Nature, flushed with fullness of incredible colour, seemed to hold her breath for the event, he looked in the very eyes of the Friend and Helper; saw the backward sweep of the curved horns, gleaming in the growing daylight; saw the stern, hooked nose between the kindly eyes that were looking down on them humorously, while the bearded mouth broke into a half-smile at the corners; saw the rippling muscles on the arm that lay across the broad chest, the long supple hand still holding the pan-pipes only just fallen away from the parted lips; saw the splendid curves of the shaggy limbs disposed in majestic ease on the sward . . .'

Little of this pre-Raphaelite enchantment gets through to the album, and the really outstanding thing about it, and the link with what was to follow, is the instrumental work, not only on the straight non-vocals ('Interstellar Overdrive') and songs where the words are not really significant ('Take Up Thy Stethoscope and Walk', 'Astronomy Domine'), but also the songs which purport to have some intelligible message to convey. For instance, it is the band's work which makes 'Lucifer Sam' more significant than it might otherwise have been.

What is notable is how kindly it has been treated by time. It is the only real evidence that Syd Barrett's reputation as an important influence on the direction of the band was at all deserved.

A Saucerful of Secrets
Prod Norman Smith, rec EMI, Abbey Road, rel June 29 1968

> Let There Be More Light (Waters)
> Remember a Day (Wright)
> Set the Controls for the Heart of the Sun (Waters)
> Corporal Clegg (Waters)
>
> A Saucerful of Secrets (Waters, Wright, Mason, Gilmour)
> See-Saw (Wright)
> Jugband Blues (Barrett)

Syd Barrett was already withdrawing from things at the time of the second album, and in fact he and Dave Gilmour shared the guitar playing between them equally.

'We played I think five or six gigs with five of us, through late January and February '68, I suppose,' recalls Dave. 'Even in those days recording tended to be a few people playing and then drop-in overdubbing afterwards. There are tracks on 'A Saucerful of Secrets' that Syd played on and I played on later, a little bit. 'Set the Controls for the Heart of the Sun', I think I played a bit on, and Syd had done the basic stuff on one of Rick's ones, I think.'

That would be 'Remember the Day', which had originally been intended for the first album, with some simple but effective slide guitar from Syd. It is a song about longing for the innocence of childhood, surprising in one so young (Rick Wright, who composed it, was then a mere 22 years old).

The album closed with Syd's 'Jugband Blues', whose disoriented single verse and chorus belied the sort of music that, presumably, inspired its title. As a farewell to the band that was to continue for another 16 years after he left, it is a chilling composition. One wonders why Peter Jenner and Andrew King had wanted it for a single. (Perhaps because it was so short?)

One of Syd's more inspired ideas was to invite a Salvation Army band into the studio to play anything they wanted in the middle section, fading in and out of the guitar noises until the sudden cut-off before Syd sings the final, paranoid words at the end of the album, his last words on record with the band. According to Miles, 'Syd Barrett, with guitar in hand, apparently sat in the reception area of EMI's Abbey Road studios for days on end waiting for the rest of the group to invite him to play more on the album.'

Though the title track was undoubtedly what set the band on its subsequent course, it has dated more than things like 'Set the Controls for the Heart of the Sun', which Waters was still able to perform with some panache at his solo concerts in the summer of '84. For instance, it doesn't bear serious comparison with Frank Zappa's 'Return of the Son of Monster Magnet' on the 'Freak Out' album which gave the expression to the language, recorded in the early hours of a March morning two years previously.

And Zappa never would have let pass anything as portentously solemn as the hymnlike chords and 'Celestial Voices' (the section's title) at the conclusion – not without making fun of it at least.

'Set the Controls' (the quote is from William S. Burroughs, of course) is altogether more significant: a bass guitar run around the cadence of the words, interspersed with barely whispered quatrains Roger found in a book of Chinese T'ang poetry (Arthur Waley? I asked, but he couldn't remember). The other significant things about the album are the two Roger Waters songs ('Set the Controls' doesn't really qualify as such), not only because the quality of the lyrics was well above anything on the first album, but because the arrangements are really well realised.

On the whole, though, it's like many second albums, not fulfilling the promise of the first and its coherence bedevilled by, and reflecting, the unease within the band.

The two albums were later packaged together as 'A Nice Pair', the cover of which had to be replaced when a dentist called W. R. Phang (dentist . . . phang . . . gettit?) objected to the window of his surgery being depicted on it. Something to do with not being allowed to advertise . . .

Today, there'd be more problem with the sexist title and naked lady on the cover.

More
Prod by Pink Floyd, rel July 1969

> Cirrus Minor (Waters)
> The Nile Song (Waters)
> Crying Song (Waters)
> Up the Khyber (Mason, Wright)
> Green is the Colour (Waters)
> Cymbaline (Waters)
> Party Sequence (Waters, Wright, Gilmour, Mason)
>
> Main Theme (Waters, Wright, Gilmour, Mason)
> Ibiza Bar (Waters, Wright, Gilmour, Mason)
> More Blues (Waters, Wright, Gilmour, Mason)
> Quicksilver (Waters, Wright, Gilmour, Mason)
> A Spanish Piece (Gilmour)
> Dramatic Theme (Waters, Wright, Gilmour, Mason)

Barbet Schroeder's 'More' was Floyd's third movie (not counting items like the C. O. I. promo for 'Jugband Blues' and a 15-minute 'Day in the life of San Francisco' documentary which had Gilmour playing on 'Interstellar Overdrive') and there was very little to choose between them as examples of filmdom's failure to understand what was going on in the underground.

First came Peter Sykes' 'The Committee', starring Manfred man Paul Jones, shown to the press but never released. A soundtrack album was rumoured – there's even been a catalogue number allocated – but that, too, never came out. Crazy World of Arthur Brown also played. Fred Dellar's description catches the interchangeable scenario of this kind of Sixties' movie: 'A hitch-hiker (Jones) beheads a thorough bore, then sews his head back on; a chilling fable exploring R. D. Laing's thesis that schizophrenia and crime are the only sane responses to a sick society.' ('NME Guide to Rock Cinema').

Peter Whitehead's gruesome (and gruesomely titled) music documentary 'Tonite Let's Make Love in London', included three sequences of 'Interstellar Overdrive' (actually three segments from the same recording), sharing the soundtrack with the likes of the Stones, Eric Burdon, Chris Farlowe and the Small Faces. The rare soundtrack album contains the full version of 'Overdrive' as used in the film, which is different from the version on 'Piper'.

Next came Schroeder's 'More' with a scenario reading much like that of 'The Committee'. Dellar, again: 'A German student in Paris is involved with drugs and a love affair with a one-time lesbian in this ludicrous melodrama that attempts to prove that speed kills.' (Heroin, actually, but the point is well taken.)

Five out of the 13 songs on the soundtrack album were by Waters, and while none of them were world-beaters, 'Cymbaline' and 'Green is the Colour' were still being included in the Floyd's live sets well into 1971. (They are, for instance available on live bootlegs recorded in Amsterdam, October 1969, England, 1970, Hamburg, 1970, and Fillmore West, New York, October 15, 1971.

The really significant thing about these movies was that they fuelled Waters' desire to produce concept albums.

Umma Gumma
Live sides (1 & 2) prod by Pink Floyd, rec Mothers, Birmingham, April 27, 1969, Chamber of Commerce, Manchester, May 2, 1969, studio sides (3 & 4) prod Norman Smith, rel Oct 25 1969

> Astronomy Domine (Barrett)
> Careful With That Axe, Eugene (Waters, Wright, Gilmour, Mason)
>
> Set the Controls for the Heart of the Sun (Waters)
> A Saucerful of Secrets: Something Else; Syncopated Pandemonium; Storm Signal; Celestial Voices (Waters, Wright, Gilmour, Mason)
>
> Sysyphus (Parts 1-4) (Wright)
> Grantchester Meadows (Waters)
> Several Species of Small Furry Animals Gathered Together in a Cave and Grooving With a Pict (Waters)

The Narrow Way (Parts 1-3) (Gilmour)
The Grand Vizier's Garden Party: Part 1-Entrance, Part 2-Entertainment, Part 3-Exit (Mason)

It's ironic that, at a time when they were probably finding it hard to think as a group, this was the first and only time the Floyd fell for the live album syndrome. All the other live recordings we have are bootlegs, and of course they are so poorly documented that any value they might have for the rock archivist is strictly limited. This is not to mention their quality, which varies from dreadful to just about acceptable.

Rick Wright was feeling out of sympathy with the kind of music the band had been making, and had some solo stuff he wanted to lay down, so it was agreed to package together a disc of live tracks with solo projects from all four. The trouble was that not all of them – Dave Gilmour, for instance – were as prolific writers as Roger and Rick.

Gilmour doesn't think a great deal of the results: 'It was just one of those things, where someone makes this suggestion of doing these solo things. I think it was Rick who wanted to do a kind of solo piece, because he was the one who tended to grumble the most about the musical direction we were going in, and all that sort of stuff. He said he wanted to make real music.

'I was not ready for it, frankly. I didn't know what to do. I just bullshitted my way through my piece on that. I got desperate at one point and rang Roger up and said "Please help me to write the lyrics", but he said "No, do 'em yourself". So I had to, but I mean it's nothing, really. Not really. I don't see it as having any real value. I've never listened to it for donkey's years, mind you, so I don't know.'

On the other hand, of course, the live sections are probably responsible for much of the Floyd myth; certainly, the four songs are what those people have in mind who say that the band didn't live up to the promise of its early days after 'Dark Side', despite their later commercial success.

The tunes come across with greater power than the studio versions, belying the band's later reputation as a group which merely re-ran the albums on stage – or perhaps explaining the anger of those who felt that was what they were doing by then. But the real difference is probably due to the inclusion of Gilmour in the ensembles: his guitar playing in his first solo on 'Astronomy Domine' indicates that the departure of Syd has *strengthened* the group's innovatory instrumental sound, not put an end to the classic Floyd.

Nick Mason said that they recorded the old tunes as a sort of farewell: 'We made "Umma Gumma" in the belief that we wouldn't have to perform those numbers any more.'

The studio tracks are less happy, and Waters' two contributions are less significant than most of the things he produced before or since, though 'Grantchester Meadows' is a reasonable enough lyric, a sort of sub-Rupert Brooke evocation of a Cambridge city pastoral:

> Hear the lark and harken to the barking of a dogfox gone
>   to ground.
> See the splashing of the Kingfisher flashing to the water
> And the river of green is sliding unseen beneath the trees
> Laughing as it passes through the endless summer making for
>   the sea.

It stayed in their repertoire for a while, to judge from the bootlegs, but it reads like a bit of juvenilia (Waters is a great hoarder of scraps of paper carrying notes of previous work) that just came in handy when they were making the album. Though the acoustic guitar lacks their facility, it sounds as if it's been influenced by the folk baroque school of English guitarists, headed by Davey Graham.

Despite his own dislike of them, Gilmour's bits aren't half bad, though his lack of confidence in his own songwriting abilities is probably the reason why the voice is mixed down so low. It doesn't compare with anything he's done before, or since, however.

The double album ends with Nick Mason's three-part exploration of electronically-processed drum sounds; Mason's connections with the avant garde (eg Mike Mantler, Robert Wyatt, Gong) were less superficial than that of the other three and though he is no Max Roach, it works well enough.

If it hadn't been for the live tracks however, the album would have been a complete write-off.

By the way, the title means 'a bit of the other', ie screwing, I'm informed. Or screwing around?

Zabriskie Point
Rel March 1970

> Heart Beat, Pig Meat
> Crumbling Land
> Come In Number 51, Your Time Is Up

In every way a chronicle of missed opportunities, Antonioni's attempt to repeat for the American 'evenements' what he'd done for Swinging London in 'Blow-Up' is an uneven, poorly realised film with some occasional pieces of magical cinematography, notably the love-making scene in the desert and the penultimate explosion sequence, the latter utilising for the purpose a reworked version of 'Careful With That Axe Eugene' called 'Come In Number 51'.

They worked on the music for two weeks, and in the end Antonioni only used three pieces, though tunes called 'Oneone', 'Fingal's Cave' and 'Rain in the Country' from the soundtrack recordings have appeared on bootlegs and 'Us and Them' became part of 'Dark Side of the Moon'.

Roger Waters described the hardships of the job to Zig-Zag magazine in 1973: 'We went to Rome and stayed in this posh hotel. Every day we would get up at about 4.30 in the afternoon, we'd pop into the bar, and sit there till about seven, then we'd stagger into the restaurant, where we'd eat for about two hours, and drink . . . the Crepes Suzette would finally slide down by about a quarter to nine.

'We'd start work at about nine; the studio was a few minutes' walk down the road, so we'd stagger down the road. We could have finished the whole thing in about five days because there wasn't too much to do. Antonioni was there and we did some great stuff, but he'd listen and go – and I remember he had this terrible twitch – he'd go: 'Eet's very beautiful, but eet's too sad' or: 'Eet's too strroong'. It was always something that stopped it being perfect. You'd change whatever was wrong and he'd still be unhappy.

'It was hell, sheer hell. He'd sit there and fall asleep every so often, and we'd go on working till about seven or eight in the morning, go back and have breakfast, go to bed, get up and then back into the bar.'

Not only did he pad out their work with tracks from the sort of predictable groups – Grateful Dead, for instance – you'd expect to find in a film about the American underground at that time, but he also got them to play 'a kind of country and western number which he could have got done better by any number of American bands' (Dave Gilmour).

'But he chose ours – very strange.'

Atom Heart Mother
Prod by Pink Floyd, rec EMI, Abbey Road, eng Peter Bown, Alan Parsons, rel Oct 10 1970

> Atom Heart Mother: (a) Father's Shout, (b) Breast Milky, (c) Mother Fore, (d) Mind Your Throats Please, (f) Remergence (Waters, Wright, Gilmour, Mason, Geesin)
>
> If (Waters)
> Summer '68 (Wright)
> Fat Old Sun (Gilmour)
> Alan's Psychedelic Breakfast: (a) Rise and Shine, (b) Sunny

GAMES FOR MAY - Pink Floyd celebrate their first recording contract on the steps of EMI's Manchester Square offices. Left to right: Nick Mason, Richard Wright, Syd Barrett, Roger Waters.
Picture: Cyrus Andrews

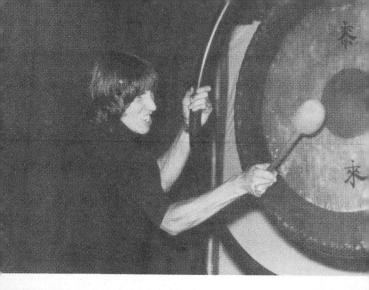

Roger gives the gong some stick at the NJF Plumpton Festival, 1969 (above) and croons at Earls Court, '73.
Pictures: Robert Ellis

Top, left: Syd just after leaving Floyd.
Picture: Barry Plummer

Dave with two of his favourite Stratocasters.
Pictures: (top, right) Kate Garner; (bottom) Robert Ellis

Top: Richard Wright at Crystal Palace, 1971
Bottom: Nick Mason with his Hokusai drum kit in Edinburgh on the "Wish You Were Here" tour, November 1974.
Pictures: Robert Ellis

Dave in the band for the Roy Harper "Unknown Soldier" tour.
Picture: EMI

Top: Floyd in full cry, especially Dave.
Picture: EMI
Bottom: Recording "Atom Heart Mother" in France with full symphony
orchestra.
Picture: Melody Maker

Top to bottom: Dave, Roger, Nick, Rick
Pictures: Karl Dallas. Robert Ellis. EMI, EMI

Dave messes with special effects at home.
Picture: Robert Ellis

Dave on his rusty steed.
Picture: Hipgnosis

Top: Nick with one of his stable of racers.
Picture: Melody Maker

Bottom: Is this the same man?
Picture: Robert Ellis

The show begins before you enter the auditorium.
Top: Outside Earls Court, 1973.
Bottom: Crazed fans risk drowning to get to their heroes at Crystal Palace.
Pictures: Robert Ellis

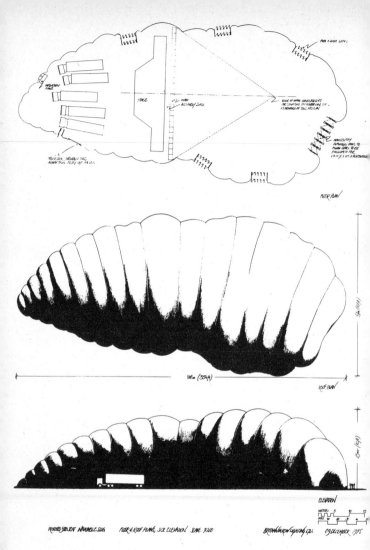

An abandoned touring project conceived during the gestation of "The Wall" was The Slug, an inflatable temporary concert hall 354 feet long and 82 feet high with seats for 3000 people in a 24,756 square feet main auditorium area, plus over 16,000 feet back stage, making a total area of over 40,000 square feet. It never happened.
Pictures from Britannia Row, the Floyd's facilities company

PROPOSED RURAL SLUG FOR THE WALL

The growth of special effects. Bottom: The plane crashes to its doom.
Pictures: Robert Ellis

Gerald Scarfe inflatables at Earls Court.
Picture: Robert Ellis

The Wall, Los Angeles, February 1980
Picture: Melody Maker

"The Wall" movie, with Bob Geldof as Pink.
Above: He scrabbles at the wall he has built around himself.
Bottom: Sitting in a surreal landscape.
Pictures: UPI (UK)

Side Up, (c) Morning Glory (Waters, Wright, Gilmour, Mason)

For a long time, Nick Mason said that 'Atom Heart Mother' was the only early Floyd he could listen to, though he also tended to accept Dave Gilmour's dismissive reminder that it was recorded in a bit of a rush. The inclusion of Ron Geesin as arranger was bound to make it sound rather different. Geesin is one of the great Scots eccentrics – Ivor Cutler is another – who live on the fringes of the rock and folk scenes.

Geesin is a year older than Waters, and had played trad piano in the Original Downtown Syncopators and made a remarkable album of electronic innovations in 1967, when he was just 23 ('A Raise of Eyebrows' on Transatlantic STRA161, if you can find it, and it's worth looking for), the sort of thing Roger was obviously trying to achieve on 'Several Species etc' on 'Umma Gumma'.

According to Nick Mason, Sam Cutler, who was to acquire dubious notoriety later as the man who hired Hells Angels to police Altamont for the Stones, introduced Geesin to Roger Waters when he was working on the music for the soundtrack of Tony ('Cathy Come Home') Garnett's 'The Body' film, directed by Roy Battersby.

As premiered in France, in January 1970, and later on the John Peel radio show, 'Atom Heart Mother' was untitled, and, before Geesin got his hands on the arrangements for orchestra and choir, was much simpler than its grandiose final form. Dave Gilmour said it was originally 'a theme for a Western with the chord sequence'. An evening newspaper had carried a headline about a pregnant woman (or her baby; the memories of different members of the band differ) who had to be kept alive with an atomic pacemaker, and the album was given its title when they had to put something down on Peel's PR sheet.

This was the raw material Geesin worked on. 'We'd got a lot of backing track, which we gave him so he knew vaguely what we were into,' says Roger Waters. 'Rick worked with him on the pieces for the people to sing and he wrote the introduction completely out of his Scottish head.'

This was the time of rock-plus-classics hybrids, Deep Purple's 'Concerto for Group and Orchestra' and suchlike nonsensical outcomes of the Sixties' obsession with its own seriousness, and after the full work was unveiled to the British public in all its self-importance at the Bath festival in June, followed by the Hyde Park free concert, the post-hippy generation took it to their hearts.

Frankly, I agree with Leonard Bernstein, who liked the rest of the album but confessed himself bored by 'Atom Heart Mother'.

It has some good, rather splendid melodies that might work as settings for the jingoistic verses of the likes of Cecil Spring-Rice (who set the words of 'I Vow to Thee, My Country' to Holst's 'Saturn', from the 'Planets' suite), and effective, mostly wordless singing by the John Aldiss choir. For most of the time, though, the playing of the band is nothing much more than any average session rhythm section could have laid down, and apart from some fleeting snatches of Gilmour guitar, echoing the cello theme, the only instrumentalist who distinguishes himself on it is Rick Wright, for whom it was originally something of a solo showcase.

The real stars of the production are the engineers, Peter Bown and Alan Parsons, who used stereo very creatively (listen to the way they move Rick's organ around like a hovering UFO during his little discordant 'space bleep' riff about three-quarters of the way through). It's even more effective on the quadraphonic mix issued in SQ later the same year; Floyd had been messing with surround sound since the days of the Azimuth Co-Ordinator at the Queen Elizabeth Hall in May '67, though then they used six speakers rather than four.

Wright's song, 'Summer '68', is the most powerful of the three individual items on the reverse. In fact, if Floyd had still been releasing singles, it might have done very well as one.

Water's 'If' is obviously close enough to his heart to find a place in his current solo repertoire – though it was interesting that he had to ask the Earls Court audience not to whistle in competition with the bird noises in the live show or they wouldn't be able to hear the words – and the recording has some nice over-reverb'd Gilmour guitar.

Gilmour's own 'Fat Old Sun' is another 'Grantchester Meadows' – type summer idyll, opening and closing with evensong church bells:

> *When that fat old sun in the sky's falling*
> *Summer evening birds are calling*
> *Summer Sunday and a year*
> *The sound of music in my ears*
> *Distant bells*
> *New mown grass smells*
> *By the river holding hands . . .*

Dave sings in a slightly falsetto voice reminiscent of Ray Davies (perhaps he'd been listening to 'Sunny Afternoon'?), and there's some exceedingly powerful guitar towards the coda, which is reminiscent of no one, but harking forward to the impact of his playing on 'Dark Side of the Moon'. 'Alan's Psychedelic Breakfast' is no better than they have indicated they think in later interviews, and in fact there had been better examples of the manipulation of actuality sounds on previous albums, especially the 'Body' soundtrack.

Again, the thing that sticks in the mind is not so much the actuality as some pretty keyboard work from Rick, floating in and out of the mix.

The real significance of 'Atom Heart Mother' was probably the fact that it was their most successful attempt at a lengthy structure in several parts. As Nick Mason said, they never could have done 'Meddle' if they hadn't first done 'Atom Heart Mother'.

Not only that but it demonstrated the power of packaging to present their music as something 'significant', from the uncaptioned Hipgnosis cover of cows to the 40ft Sunset Strip billboards which greeted them in Los Angeles when they toured the States to promote the album. This wasn't the first time Hipgnosis had worked on their productions: the same company did the solarised cover of 'More' and the picture-within-a-picture puzzle cover of 'Umma Gumma', but from now until 'Wish You Were Here', Hipgnosis were to be an essential ingredient of the Floyd experience. The home listener couldn't see the special effects and animated projections that were an increasingly important part of the live shows – not until video, anyway – but you could always ponder on the sleeve as you listened, couldn't you?

Meddle
Prod by Pink Floyd, rec at AIR and EMI, Abbey Road, eng Peter Bown, John Leckie, and at Morgan, eng Bob Black and Roger Quested, Jan, Mar, April, May, Aug 1971, rel Nov 1971

> One of These Days (Waters, Wright, Gilmour, Mason)
> A Pillow of Winds (Waters, Gilmour)
> Fearless (Waters, Gilmour)
> San Tropez (Waters)
> Seamus (Waters, Wright, Gilmour, Mason)
>
> Echoes (Waters, Wright, Gilmour, Mason)

'"Meddle" was the first sign really of having a direction and knowing and trying to achieve something. I mean the track "Echoes" on "Meddle" definitely for me achieved something very good and strong, although the lyrics aren't something that Roger would put down on the list of his top five lyrics ever.

'Well, I can't really remember the lyrics on "Echoes" itself as being that significant. There are songs on that album that are more significant, I think, I can't remember the titles, the one with "You'll Never Walk

101

Alone" on the end of it. I think there are things on that album that pointed towards the direction that Roger was going to want to move into.' (Dave Gilmour)

The song whose title Dave couldn't remember was 'Fearless'.

> *You say the hill's too steep to climb,*
> *Climbing,*
> *You say you'd like to see me try,*
> *Climbing,*
> *You pick the place and I'll choose the time,*
> *And I'll climb the hill in my own way*
> *Just wait awhile for the right day*
> *And as I rise above the treeline and the clouds*
> *I look down and hear the sound of the things you said today.*

It's a good song in its own right, direct though allusive, employing concrete images in a way that nevertheless suggests peripheral vision rather than a hard-edged spotlight, but the cross fading with the football crowd as the open-tuned G-major guitar continues with the background riff makes it a really powerful statement about persistence and the strength of being human.

The fact that the second verse could be referring to Syd (*Fearlessly the idiot faced the crowd*) adds to its poignancy.

The basic album was recorded in three three-day sessions at EMI in January. 'We booked the studio for January and through January we went in and played, any time that anyone had any sort of rough idea for something we could put down,' said Dave. 'It was a specific attempt to sort of do something by a slightly different method.' One of the things they used to do, apparently, was to decide on a key then all but one leave the room, while the one left would play what he liked. 'Absolute rubbish!' said Dave.

However, during that 'messing about' they discovered the echoey note that opens and closes 'Echoes', by putting a piano note through a Binson echo unit. 'By the end of January,' added Dave, 'we listened back and we'd got 36 different bits and pieces that sometimes cross-related and sometimes didn't. 'Echoes' was made up from that.' Despite the piecemeal construction, it was a piece that worked particularly well live; it features significantly in the 'Live at Pompeii' film, and was often used as a closing encore.

It was actually the first real masterpiece the band had produced, a lengthy work (the entire second side of the LP) that never drags and is virtually without a flaw, throughout its shifting tempi and images of floating albatrosses and strangers passed in city streets. Despite Dave's slighting reference to its lyric, Roger can still quote it from memory if you press him for the sources of the alienation theme in his work.

For once, the other side lives (almost) up to this standard for at least half the time. 'One of These Days (I'm Going to Cut You Up Into Little Pieces)' opens the album and establishes a link with the great freak-outs of 'Interstellar Overdrive' and 'Careful With That Axe, Eugene'. After its paranoid sounds, the airy dreaminess of 'Pillow of Winds' is very refreshing; proof that Floyd could write effectively about other things than angst.

The second half is a bit of a let-down, with the lightweight cocktail jazz number, 'San Tropez', completely out of context with anything Floyd ever recorded (except, possibly, 'Pow R. Toc H.' on the first album), and the jokey blues, 'Seamus', accompanied by a dog's howling.

As Dave confessed later, '"Seamus" was fun but I don't know whether we ought to have done it in the way we did it on that album really, 'cause I guess it wasn't really as funny to anybody else as it was to us.'

The artistic success of 'Meddle', and especially 'Echoes' alerted them to the danger of working to a Floyd formula. 'There are various things in the construction that have a Pink Floyd flavour,' said Nick Mason, 'but also very dangerous Pink Floyd clichés. One is the possible tendency to get stuck into a sort of slow four tempo. And the other thing is to take a melody line and flog it to death. Maybe we'll play it once slow and quiet, the next time a bit harder and the third time really heavy which tends to come a little into "Meddle" and in "Atom Heart Mother", but it's slightly more forgiveable with the choir and orchestra 'cause it's nice building an orchestra and bringing in extra bass and playing more complex lines.'

The ambitions implicit in these words were to be more than realised in the next 14 years.

Obscured by Clouds
Soundtrack music from 'La Vallee', dir Barbet Schroeder
Prod by Pink Floyd, rec Chateau d'Herouville, Paris, Feb 23-39 1972, rel June 3, 1972

> Obscured by Clouds (Waters, Gilmour)
> When You're In (Waters, Wright, Gilmour, Mason)
> Burning Bridges (Wright, Waters)
> The Gold It's In The . . . (Waters, Gilmour)
> Wot's . . . Uh the Deal (Waters, Gilmour)
> Mudmen (Wright, Gilmour)

Childhood's End (Gilmour)
Free Four (Waters)
Stay (Wright, Waters)
Absolutely Curtains (Waters, Wright, Gilmour, Mason)

Taken out of its film context, this is hardly the Floyd's greatest album ever, though it does show at least one important development in Roger Waters' inspiration.

Dave Gilmour recalls: 'On the "Obscured by Clouds" film soundtrack album there are one or two significant things. "Free Four" for example has got all the stuff about his father being killed, and *buried like a mole in a foxhole* or something, and *everyone's still on the run*, which is where all this "Wall" and "Final Cut" stuff came from.'

Dave does himself less than justice, for his own contribution was not inconsiderable, including a very fine opening song on side two of the soundtrack album, presumably inspired by the Arthur C. Clarke story of the same name, in which the author ran through some of the same ideas that surfaced later as '2001 Space Odyssey'.

It's also notable for the new maturity that came into Gilmour's own singing, especially on 'Wot's . . . Uh' on the first side, where he seems to be having a dry run for the 'Wish You Were Here' songs.

Strangely, as far as I can recall, 'Free Four' never featured in Floyd's live set, though 'Childhood's End' crops up on a French bootleg recorded at the time.

The other noteworthy thing about the band's playing is that they are developing their ability to make very atmospheric sounds – the opening track is a very good example – but since they have to be subservient to the screen image, they really seem to lead nowhere off the screen. It was good practice for what was to come, though.

It was not a significant contribution to the film art. Once again, Fred Dellar's laconic capsule review says it all: 'Pretty-pretty hippiness involving a wealthy longhair and his friends, who search New Guinea for a hidden valley, going native en route. How radical, how chic.'

The Dark Side of the Moon
Prod by Pink Floyd, rec at EMI, Abbey Road, June, Oct 1972, Jan, Feb 1973, eng Alan Parsons, ass Peter James, mixed Chris Thomas and (quad version) Alan Parsons, rel Mar 24 1973
Backing vocs Doris Troy, Leslie Duncan, Barry St John, vocs on 'The Great Gig in the Sky' Clare Torry, sax on 'Us and Them' and 'Money' Dick Parry

Speak to Me (Mason)
Breathe (Waters, Gilmour, Wright)

On the Run (Gilmour, Waters)
Time (Waters, Wright, Gilmour, Mason)
The Great Gig in the Sky (Wright)

Money (Waters)
Any Colour You Like (Gilmour, Mason, Wright)
Brain Damage (Waters)
Eclipse (Waters)
All lyrics Roger Waters

Almost as if to demonstrate one of the album's themes, represented in the song, 'Money', its promotion began with a row over the press reception, which had been planned at the London Planetarium. Nick Mason told Zig-Zag a few months later: 'The intention was to have the Planetarium with a quadraphonic mix, which I would have been into, but there wasn't a quadraphonic mix, there was only a stereo mix, and they'd got the most terrible speakers.'

Added Roger Waters: 'The only point of it was to make a really first-class presentation of a quadraphonic mix of the album, so that it was something special. We didn't have time to do a quadraphonic mix so we said: 'You can't do it'. But EMI wanted to do something so they went ahead.

'Nicky and Dave and I thought that it was so daft that we tried to get it stopped, and when they refused to stop it, we refused to go to it. I think it was pathetic.

'It was just stupid. They spent a lot of hot air trying to get us to go to it, but we just said: "We think it's a bad idea, we don't want to do it, we don't want to know. Obviously we couldn't stop them doing it, but I thought it was daft.'

In pique, EMI put up cardboard cut-outs of the band in the foyer to 'welcome' the press, which of course gave the hacks a field-day with snide remarks. ('I couldn't tell the cardboard ones from the real thing,' quipped one into his Bacardi hand.)

A quad mix of the album was released later.

The album itself seemed like something the band had been preparing for since their beginnings seven years before: the use of actuality recordings, the atmospheric sounds of guitar and organ and the new synthesizers, the mix of speech and song, all adding up to a concept that was masterly in its form, the controlled rage of its passion, and the affirmation of human values against everything that conspires against them in life.

Before Roger Waters brought in the lyrics of the title song when they assembled in Broadcast Gardens, West Hampstead for rehearsals in January of '73, the only thing they had was 'Us and Them', originally written for 'Zabriskie Point'. They had only six weeks to go before they were due to start touring.

Dave Gilmour recalls: 'We sat in a rehearsal room and Roger came up with the specific idea of dealing with all the things that drive people mad.'

'We went to somewhere in West Hampstead for a couple of weeks and got a lot of little pieces together,' added Roger. 'No lyrics – like the riff of "Money" came out of it. There was a meeting in Nicky's kitchen and I said: 'You want a theme that runs through it, life with a heartbeat an' that. Then you can have other bits, like all the pressures which are anti-life . . .'

Much of Roger's feelings may have spilled over from his work with Ron Geesin on 'The Body', Tony Garnett's remarkably humanistic movie which combined documentary discussions, internal micro-cinematography, and some rather impressionistic romantic sequences (like your actual unsimulated copulation) into a very positive statement about the value of life.

Indeed, the opening words of the 'Dark Side' album, *Breathe, breathe in the air* were also included in the first lyric for 'The Body', even though the song's melody and later lyrics are quite different.

I've never had a chance to ask Roger how much his thinking was influenced by his work on 'The Body', though he has suggested he doesn't think much of the lyrics he produced at that time. But in its humanistic stance, especially a speech by Peter Kerrigan about the necessity of fighting for people's dignity as human beings, it shared a great deal with the ideas behind all Roger's later lyrics.

And in its exposure of the naked beauty of *all* human beings, the black lady with the fat belly and the old woman with pendulous breasts as well as the inevitable blonde beauty who had hang-ups about baring her all (and kept her pants on, while everyone else shed theirs), it was a valuable alternative to the 'beautiful people' syndrome of the time, and much more effective than Yoko Ono's 'bottoms' film.

One of the most exciting songs on the 'Dark Side' album is 'Money', not only in its use of edited recordings of cash registers to generate the basic 7/4 beat of the tune, but also in his heavily ironic dismissal of the values of the market economy:

> *Money get back*
> *I'm alright Jack keep your hands offa my stack*
> *Money it's a hit*
> *Don't give me none of that do-goody-good bullshit*
> *I'm in the hi-fidelity first class travelling set*
> *And I think I need a Lear jet.*

Nick said of it: 'I think it works very well and the interesting thing about that is that when Roger wrote it, it more or less all came up in the first day.'

'Yeah', agreed the composer, 'it was just a tune around those sevens, and I knew that there had to be a song about money in the piece, and I thought that the tune could be a song about money, and having decided that, it was extremely easy to make up a seven-beat intro that went well with it. I often think that the best ideas are the most obvious ones, and that's a fantastically obvious thing to do, and that's why it sounds good.'

Nevertheless, just as people were to persist in not seeing the satire behind casting human beings as animals two years later, the irony of the song's testimony to the invigorating effect of money was being lost on listeners.

Dave Gilmour said they'd tried to make the lyrics 'as simple and direct as possible'.

'And yet,' he said in some irritation, 'as we were writing them, we knew they'd be misunderstood. We still get people coming up to us who think that "Money, it's a gas" is a direct and literal statement that "We like money".'

Nine years later, interviewers were still puzzling over the implications of the final words of the last song:

> and everything under the sun is in tune
> but the sun is eclipsed by the moon

It's remarkable how patient the not notably patient Roger Waters was with the question: 'I don't see it as a riddle. The album uses the sun and the moon as symbols: the light and the dark; the good and the bad; the life force as opposed to the death force. I think it's a very simple statement saying that all the good things life can offer are there for us to grasp, but that the influence of some dark force in our natures prevents us from seizing them. The song addresses the listener and says that if you, the listener, are affected by that force, and if that force is a worry to you, well I feel exactly the same too.

'The line *I'll see you on the dark side of the moon* is me speaking to the listener, saying: 'I know you have these bad feelings and impulses because I do too and one of the ways I can make direct contact with you is to share with you the fact that I feel bad sometimes.'

At the end of '74, over a year after it was issued, Rick Wright was meditating on the success of the album.

'It's changed me in many ways,' he said, 'because it's brought in a lot of money and one feels very secure when you can sell an album for two years. But it hasn't changed my attitude to music.

'Even though it was so successful, it was made in the same way as all

107

our other albums, and the only criterion we have about releasing music is whether we like it or not. It was not a deliberate attempt to make a commercial album. It just happened that way.

'We knew it had a lot more melody than previous Floyd albums and there was a concept that ran all through it. The music was easier to absorb and having girls singing away added a commercial touch that none of our other records had.'

In 1975 Roger Waters commented on commercialism and success in relation to an interview with a member of Genesis that he'd just read.

'There was a whole bunch of stuff about how if you're listening to a Genesis album you really have to sit down and *listen*, it's not just wallpaper, not just high-class muzak like Pink Floyd or 'Tubular Bells', and I thought: "Yeah, I remember all that years ago, when nobody was buying what we were doing. We were all heavily into the notion that it was good music, Good with a capital G, and of course people weren't buying it because people don't buy good music." I may be quite wrong but my theory is that if Genesis ever start selling large quantities of albums now that Peter Gabriel – their Syd Barrett, if you like – has left, the young man who gave the interview will realise he's reached some kind of end, in terms of whatever he was striving for and all that stuff about Good Music is a load of fucking bollocks. That's my feeling anyway.'

Perhaps the most ominous pointers to what was to come came from Rick Wright and Nick Mason.

Rick: 'I like to think this hasn't put a pressure on us in terms of what we write next, but for a whole year we never did anything. We all sat around and got heavily into our reasons for being in a group. We got into a bad period when we didn't do anything at all creatively.'

Nick: 'There was a point after "Dark Side" where we might easily have broken up. Well, we'd reached all the goals rock bands tend to aim for. Perhaps we were a bit nervous about carrying on . . .'

Wish You Were Here
Prod by Pink Floyd, rec EMI, Abbey Road, Jan 6-July 1975, eng Brian Humphries, ass Peter James, rel Sept 15 1975
Voc on 'Have a Cigar' Roy Harper, backing vocs Venetta Fields and Carlena Williams, sax on 'Shine On You Crazy Diamond' Dick Parry

> Shine On You Crazy Diamond, parts 1-5 (Waters, Wright, Gilmour)
> Welcome to the Machine (Waters)
>
> Have a Cigar (Waters)
> Wish You Were Here (Waters, Gilmour)

Shine On You Crazy Diamond, parts 6-8 (Waters, Wright, Gilmour), part 9 (Wright)
All lyrics Roger Waters

Everyone thought the album was about Syd Barrett, but that's only partly true of the most obvious song reference, 'Shine On You Crazy Diamond'. Roger told me: 'That song is about him. The whole of the record was about absence of one sort or another, and his madness was one great striking example.

'Well, it's about him and it's about us all, really. It could equally have been called "Wish *We* Were Here", if you like. In the band we were going through one of our communication troughs at that point, a divergence of opinion about what we should be doing, what records should be about. I remember what was to become "Dogs" was part of that. We'd been performing it on stage, called "Raving and Drooling", and I remember Dave and I disagreeing about whether that should be on the record.'

The general consensus seems to be that it's not quite such a good album as its predecessor (how could it be? it didn't shift so many units), and it would be natural if it wasn't, considering the state that the band were in at the time.

Nick said: 'We were all rather badly mentally ill. When we were putting that one together we were all completely exhausted.'

That was hardly surprising, too, because the touring and the recording ran almost concurrently. They toured Britain between November 4 and December 14, taking the afternoon of the last day off to see Bristol City beat Notts Forest 1:0 at home. They were in the studio on January 6, 7, 8, 9, February 3, 4, 5, 6, and March 3, before they were off on a North American tour: Vancouver . . . Seattle . . . San Francisco (two nights) . . . Denver . . . Tucson . . . Phoenix . . . San Diego . . . Los Angeles (five nights). Back in the studio May 5, 6, 7, 8, and 9, and June 2, 3 and 5, then back to the States: Atlanta . . . Maryland (two nights) . . . Philadelphia (two nights) . . . Jersey City . . . New York (two nights) . . . Boston . . . Pittsburg . . . Milwaukee . . . Detroit . . . Montreal . . . Toronto.

Then it was Knebworth on July 5 and two weeks more in the studio to wrap it up: 27½ days in the studio in all and 27 North American concerts plus a major open-air spectacle back home, and all in the first seven months of the year.

No wonder Roger said he found it 'very unpleasant, unnerving and upsetting' and started thinking of building a polythene wall between the band and the audience.

Things weren't helped by a major technical foul-up in the studio, the full story of which was told by engineer Brian Humphries when I got him to première the quad mix of the album at the 1975 Audio Fair and we played the 'lost Floyd tapes' from the recording sessions.

As Dave Gilmour remembered it: 'We originally did the backing track over the course of several days, but we came to the conclusion that it just wasn't good enough. So we did it again in one day flat and got it a lot better. Unfortunately, nobody understood the desk properly and when we played it back we found that someone had switched the echo returns from monitors to tracks one and two. That affected the tom-toms and guitars and keyboard, which were playing along at the time. There was no way of saving it, so we just had to do it yet again.

'First of all we did a basic track of "Shine On You Crazy Diamond" from the beginning where the first guitar solo starts, right through to "Shine On". That was in all 20 minutes long, which was at one time going to be the whole of one side of the album. However, as we worked on it and extended it and then extracted things, we came to the decision that we would make that into the whole album and we began to work on the new stuff to slot in.'

Roger said: 'Once we accepted that we were going to go off on a tangent during the sessions it did become exciting, for me anyway, because then it was a desperate fucking battle trying to make it good. Actually, we expended too much energy before that point in order to be able to quite do it. By the time we were finishing it, after the second American tour, I hadn't got an ounce of creative energy left in me, and those last couple of weeks were a real fucking struggle.'

They'd been doing 'Shine On' live, and it was quite a marathon: the version bootlegged at the Trentham Gardens, Stoke, clocks in at just over 22 minutes. Roger decided that it should be separated into two, and they should open and close the album with the two halves.

'When we got into the studio, January '75, we started recording, and it got very laborious and tortured, and everybody seemed to be very bored by the whole thing. We pressed on regardless of the general ennui for a few weeks and then things came to a bit of a head. I felt that the only way I could retain interest in the project was to try and make the album relate to what was going on there and then, the fact that no one was really looking each other in the eye, and that it was all very mechanical, most of what was going on.

'So I suggested we change it, that we didn't do the other two songs' (presumably 'Sheep', also known as 'Raving and Drooling', and 'Dogs', alias 'You Gotta Be Crazy') 'but tried somehow to make a bridge between the first and second halves of "Shine On", and bridge them with stuff that had some kind of relevance to the state we were all in at the time. Which is how "Welcome to the Machine", "Wish You Were Here", and "Have a Cigar" came in.'

'Have a Cigar' had been written in its entirety before Roger introduced it to the rest. So was 'Welcome to the Machine'. 'Wish You Were Here' was just lyrics without a tune, which is unusual for the Floyd. Usually they have either a tune without words or words and music to start.

Roger's voice was under quite a bit of strain. On 'Machine' they actually cheated, by slowing down the tape and recording the vocal half a semitone lower than it would play back. And they asked Roy Harper, who was recording his masterful 'HQ' album at Abbey Road at the same time, to handle 'Have a Cigar' for Roger.

The album opens with a long (more than four whole minutes) slow, organ chord, with trumpet-like synthesizer notes played against it; then, after almost two minutes of this, Gilmour's guitar takes up a poignant melody; nearly two more minutes later, as the chord fades into the background, Dave plays the repeated four-note phrase (percussion crescendo) leading into and played under his own superbly moving guitar solo. The guitar tone roughens and becomes more strident, the synth sounds return, more French horn-like this time, Rick returns the lead to Dave, who develops the feeling of his first choruses two more times; then, more than 8½ minutes in from the edge, the first vocal lines hit the ear: *You remember when you were young, you shone like the sun . . .*

After seven years, his old colleagues were aiming a salute at Syd, and it was the most affectionate, most respectful, most moving tribute to an ex-member in the turbulent history of rock break-ups and make-ups. Dick Parry's impassioned sax in the coda and fade-out linked the song to the first slice of meat in the 'Shine On' sandwich, the synth-dominated 'Welcome to the Machine'.

Here, they were really living up to their (till then more or less unjustified) reputation for electronic innovation.

'It's very much a made-up-in-the-studio thing,' said Dave, 'which was all built up from a basic throbbing made on a VCS3, with a repeat echo to give the throb. With a number like that, you don't start off with a regular concept of group structure or anything, and there's no backing track either. Really, it is just a studio proposition where we're using tape for its own end, a form of collage using sound.'

The band didn't amplify the synthesizer and mike the speaker cabinet; they direct-injected its signal into the studio desk to minimise loss of the basic human 'sound'.

Though it is effective on record, what made the live performances really powerful were the animated graphics, starting with the metal dinosaur, the sea of blood that becomes an ocean of grasping hands and arms, crawling up a monolith, and then subsides, leaving the stone suspended in mid-air, before it lifts off, vanishing into space.

After the long drawn-out, almost long-winded instrumental opening of the first side, the straightforward single bluesy chorus which opens side two with 'Have a Cigar' is almost a shock. The singer is Roy Harper, in typically one-man-rock 'n'roll-band style, and the intrusion of a less familiar voice works a similar magic to that of Clare Torry on the previous album.

Harper was Roger's idea, but he confesses that he wanted to be talked out of it. 'I sort of expected them to say, "No, you do it, Roger", but they didn't. They said: "Great idea!" Now I wish that I had done it.

'A lot of people think I can't sing, including me a bit. I'm very unclear about what singing is. I know I find it hard to pitch, and I know the sound of my voice isn't very good in purely aesthetic terms. Roy Harper was recording his own album in another EMI studio at the time, he's a mate, and we thought he could probably do a job on it.'

I wonder how many first-time buyers have anxiously checked their system during Gilmour's solo at the end of the track, which sounds as if their output stage has suddenly blown. It's all part of the sound mix, however. You might think the title song is definitely all about Syd, despite Roger's disclaimers, but to judge by what he told Nick Sedgwick, there's more to this particular lyric than meets the ear.

'In a way it's a schizophrenic song. It's directed at my other half, if you like, the battling elements within myself. There's the bit that's concerned with other people, the bit that one applauds in oneself, then there's the grasping, avaricious, selfish little kid who wants to get his hands on the sweets and have them all. The song slips in and out of both personae so the bit that always wants to win is feeling upset and plaintively saying to the other side, *wish you were here*.

'And later, in 'The Wall', I've tried to communicate the idea that the relationship we've had between us, between "us" in our lead role on stage, and "them", the audience, has been a false one which neither of us has entirely understood.'

The reprise of 'Shine On' ends the album as it started, with Rick Wright's synthesizer, and improvisation leads subtly into 'Strangers in the Night', ending the album on a witty yet poignantly appropriate note.

Animals
Prod by Pink Floyd, rec at Britannia Row, London, April-Nov 1976, rel Feb 4 1977

  Pigs on the Wing 1 (Waters)
  Dogs (Waters, Gilmour)

Pigs (Three Different Ones) Waters
Sheep (Waters)
Pigs on the Wing 2 (Waters)

'Animals' did not receive a good reception. It was partly, that bad old media game of turning against past success, and partly that the megasales of its two predecessors gave something of a shock to those who thought everyone should die before they got old.

In some ways too, it was a refusal to see that in categorising human beings as animals, Roger Waters was not denying the value of our humanity any more than Orwell's 'Animal Farm' was consigning us to the farmyard. I have no reason to revise the judgement I made at the time, that, contrary to what the *Rolling Stone* magazine was still asserting five years later, it was saying something positive rather than negative about our humanity, despite what Roger had called 'pressures which are anti-life'.

Here's what I wrote about it the week before it was released (perhaps, to put the opening paragraphs in context, it should be realised that this was immediately after EMI's notorious cancellation of the Sex Pistols' contract):

> Here is a memo to Sir John Read, head of the EMI group. You are about to release an album which features obscenity, profanity and a dastardly attack upon a well-known public figure.
>
> But before you consider cancelling your contract with them, perhaps you should know that it is by one of your best-selling bands, whose last two albums have hogged the album charts for months at a time, and it is my prediction that this one will repeat that pattern. It is, in short, Pink Floyd's long-awaited follow-up to 1973's 'Dark Side of the Moon' and 1975's 'Wish You Were Here'.
>
> I'd also venture to predict that, just as the last two earned a degree of critical dismay inversely proportions to both records' eventual success, this new release will be greeted, once again, by loud cries for the return of Syd Barrett; despite which the punters will buy it by the million. Me, I like it, but then never having been a hardcore Floyd freak until 'Meddle' indicated their increasing mastery of studio technology and ability to play the mixing board like it was a fifth instrument, I may be in a critical minority of one.
>
> In a sense, the new album forms the third part of a trilogy, in which the theme of alienation ('Dark Side') and loneliness ('Wish') is wrapped up by an intense and savage humanism,

which is paradoxically all the more powerful by being personified in a series of animal caricatures.

While the Bible separates people into sheep and goats, this Floyd work divides them three ways: dogs, pigs, and sheep. The three sections are sandwiched between the first and second verses of an acoustic song, 'Pigs on the Wing', sung by Waters in a neo-Sixties singer-songwriter style that is so alien to everything one associates with the Floyd that it comes like a douche of cold water to clear the mind for what follows. In itself, it is not really a great song by any standards, but in context it serves a definite purpose, as a sort of moral framework to the often horrific lyrics in between.

The rest of side one is devoted to 'Dogs', a horrendous depiction of the modern world as 'nature red in tooth and claw', the dogs of the acquisitive society rending each other, retiring into loneliness and dying of cancer or dragged down to death by *the weight you used to need to throw around*.

There is a moment about two-thirds of the way through the song when Waters' singing of the phrase *dragged down by the stone* is put on to a tape loop and repeated almost ad nauseam, while the human overtones of the voice are gradually filtered out, till at the end it becomes little more than a high-pitched howl, like a cry heard through deep water.

Meanwhile, the band takes the recurring phrase as the ground rhythm for a long instrumental, and the sound of barking dogs is processed through a sort of effects box called a Vocoder, creating semi-musical chords out of them, while still retaining their doggy character. A chilling moment, which managed to reach me the first time I heard it, during the fuggy chat of the Battersea Park play-through.

'Pigs (Three Different Ones)' opens side two with very unflattering portraits of modern figures, each of them laughed to scorn, including a *house-proud town mouse* called Whitehouse, *trying to keep our feelings off the street*, which sketches in with a few deft moves, a picture of the censorious Mary as frustrated married spinster, *all tight lips and cold feet*. There is a line of heavy breathing on her verse, which I suspect is a censored version of something even less flattering, since it is followed by a shout of 'you!'

Even in these savage attacks, however, there is an element of pity, for each of the three victims of Floyd's ire is described as *really a cry*, rather than the laugh the lyric pretends at first to have at their expense.

'Sheep' is almost a mini 'Animal Farm', a picture of the contented mass, grazing peacefully on their way to the slaughterhouse. Again, there is a chilling moment when a grim parody of the 23rd Psalm

with bright knives He releaseth my soul
He maketh me to hang on hooks in high places
He converteth me to lamb chops

is intoned through the Vocoder. This doesn't make the horror any easier to take, but it does integrate the intrusion musically, though possibly a little less processing or more up-front mixing might have brought this section out more strongly.

The sheep revolt, killing the dogs, but the words *march cheerfully out of obscurity into the dream* suggest that perhaps this is the only part of the album not entirely rooted in reality. And is the whole thing, like the story of the canine heroes in Clifford Simak's SF epic, 'City', merely a fable told by one dog to another? There is a definite suggestion that the characters huddling together for shelter from pigs on the wing in the reprise of the opening acoustic song are dogs as well.

So much for the lyrical content, which is easier to talk about than the extremely thick mix of music, at times multi-layered and at others deceptively simple. Apart from the startling open and close, which is as shocking as a common chord of C in the middle of a piece of atonal music, the tunes are thematically very close to those of the previous two albums, with a number of tunes based on a rising minor second interval.

But while, in the other two, it was possible to ignore the somewhat convoluted implications of the lyrics, treating the rich textures as a rather superior kind of musical wallpaper, here the savagery of the words is, at times, rather too close for this kind of complacent comfort, and the music only serves to underline the significance of the lyrics.

For that reason, perhaps, the album may not be as commercially successful as the others, for at times the shocks come as staggeringly as Johnny Rotten gobbing at his audience, an uncomfortable taste of reality in a medium ('progressive' rock) that has become in recent years increasingly soporific. It is almost as if the Floyd realised that a lot of their buyers had managed to doze their way through the implications of the previous albums, and were determined to ensure that it didn't happen the third time round.

Perhaps they should rename themselves Punk Floyd.

Nine years later, I am not inclined to modify that high estimate. I still think the opening and closing songs are weak, a verdict which was confirmed by the reaction of the crowd to 'Pigs on the Wing' at Waters' '84 solo concerts, for some reason the only song from this immensely powerful and moving album which he performed. Perhaps the other songs were too long.

On the other hand, though, it was extremely brave of the band to end the album on such a low-key note rather than on a rousing finish, which is the obvious rabble-rousing crowd-pleasing rock tradition. They've done it since, of course, with subsequent albums, and it continues to be a brave break with convention, but this was the first time. As we have seen, the ideas and images that became, first, 'Animals', and then 'The Wall', were germinating in Roger Waters' mind at the time of the 1972-3 'Dark Side' tour, and some of the 'Animals' songs were given try-outs in subsequent years' tours.

After the Frankfurt opening for the promotional tour that immediately followed the release of the album, Nick Mason agreed with me that the new work was the culmination of the previous two. 'Of course,' he said, 'but we didn't plan it that way. But it just seemed that with "Dark Side" we somehow got lucky, and things began to fall into place in a way they hadn't before.

'This one is really my favourite. I've never been able to listen to any of our previous albums once we've finished them because we've spent so much time with them that there's no pleasure in it. But, with the possible exception of "Saucer", this is the only one I like playing.'

Later, though, in 1982 Roger told me that I wasn't quite right with my 'trilogy' theory: 'Animals' was really the first part of 'The Wall' (and I suppose 'The Final Cut' and elements of 'Hitch-hiking' were the conclusion).

'I think "Animals" is more to do with "The Wall" than with "Wish You Were Here",' he said. 'In fact, when I started jotting ideas down, strange ideas for a film, at one time, I did a lot of drawings using animal masks and things.'

DALLAS: 'This was after "The Wall" album but when you were working on the movie?'

'No, No, no, no. I was working on ideas for the movie even before I started writing music for "The Wall".'

That same year, Roger was dismissing 'Animals' as 'a bit thrown together'.

116

'There aren't enough songs on it,' he told Nick Sedgwick, 'and the ones that are there are rather too long. "Sheep" was a song called "Raving and Drooling" which was intended to be on "Wish You Were Here" but I didn't think it was right. It was therefore left over. "Pigs" was written a couple of years earlier. I'm not sure about "Dogs"; it was Dave's chord sequence left over from "Wish You Were Here", I think. It wasn't until we were recording those three pieces it occurred to me that they could be cobbled together under the title "Animals" and they were descriptive, anthropomorphic ideas.

'I think one of the songs stands up: "Sheep". It was my sense of what was to come down in England and it did last summer with the riots in England, in Brixton and Toxteth . . .'

SEDGWICK: 'Where did that sense come from?'

'Probably that it had happened before in Notting Hill in the early Sixties. And it will happen again. It will always happen. There are too many of us in the world and we treat each other badly. We get obsessed with things and there aren't enough things, products, to go round. If we're persuaded it's important to have them, that we're nothing without them, and there aren't enough of them to go round, the people without them are going to get angry. Content and discontent follow very closely the rise and fall on the graph of world recession and expansion.

'I think the thing about "Animals" was that it didn't jel cohesively either musically or conceptually, but perhaps that was good. Three fairly angry songs about the posturing and defensive ploys set between two verses of a love song to Carolyne' (his second wife) '"Pigs on the Wing". The first verse poses the question: "Where would I be without you?" and the second verse says "in the face of all this other shit – confusion, sidetracks, difficulties – you care, I know you care about me and that makes it possible to survive". That is the first time that sentiment appears, the sense of having somebody, being with somebody.'

It is still an important sentiment, as the final words of 'The Pro's and Cons of Hitch-hiking' show.

PART THREE
The Wall Itself

THE WALL

The Album
Prod by David Gilmour, Bob Ezrin, Roger Waters, co-prod & eng by James Guthrie, Nick Griffiths, Patrice Quef, Brian Christian, Rick Hart, John McClure, rec at Super Bear, Miravel, France, CBS, New York, Producers' Workshop, Los Angeles, April–Nov 1979, rel Nov 30 1979
Backing vocs Bruce Johnston, Toni Tennille, Joe Chemay, John Joyce, Stan Farber, Jim Haas, Islington Green School fourth form music class
Orch arrs by Michael Kamen & Bob Ezrin

> In the Flesh? (Waters)
> The Thin Ice (Waters)
> Another Brick in the Wall, Part 1 (Waters)
> The Happiest Days of Our Lives (Waters)
> Another Brick in the Wall, Part 2 (Waters)
> Mother (Waters)
>
> Goodbye Blue Sky (Waters)
> Empty Spaces (Waters)
> Young Lust (Gilmour, Waters)
> One of My Turns (Waters)
> Don't Leave Me Now (Waters)
> Another Brick in the Wall, Part 3 (Waters)
> Goodbye, Cruel World (Waters)
>
> Hey You (Waters)
> Is There Anybody Out There? (Waters)
> Nobody Home (Waters)
> Vera (Waters)
> Bring the Boys Back Home (Waters)
> Comfortably Numb (Waters)
>
> The Show Must Go On (Waters)
> In the Flesh (Waters)
> Run Like Hell (Gilmour, Waters)
> Waiting for the Worms (Waters)
> Stop (Waters)
> The Trial (Waters, Ezrin)
> Outside the Wall (Waters)

The Movie, the Video

An Alan Parker film, PINK FLOYD THE WALL, by Roger Waters, designed by Gerald Scarfe

Music written by Roger Waters, exc 'Comfortably Numb', 'Young Lust', 'Run Like Hell' (written with David Gilmour), 'The Trial' (written with Bob Ezrin)

Additional musicians and singers: Andy Bown, Bobby Hall, Jess & Joe Porcaro, Willie Wilson, Freddie Mandell, Bob Ezrin, Lee Ritenour, Bruce Johnstone, Tony Tenille, Joe Chemay, Stan Farber, Jim Haas, Jon Joyce, Islington Green School Choir, Pontardulais Male Voice Choir led by Noel Davis, 'The Little Boy That Santa Claus Forgot' sung by Vera Lynn

Made at Pinewood Studios, London, England, by Tin Blue Ltd in association with Goldcrest Films

Rel July 14 1982

Cert 'AA', length 8571 ft, running time 1 hour 35 mins

The Official Synopsis of the Film

Pink, a Rock and Roll performer, sits locked in a hotel room, somewhere in Los Angeles. Too many shows, too much dope, too much applause; a burned out case. On the TV, an all too familiar war film flickers on the screen. We shuffle time and place, reality and nightmare, as we venture into Pink's painful memories and inevitably into his madness.

Our hero is a baby born in the Second World War at the same time as his father is killed in action at the Battle of Anzio, and so Pink grows up never knowing him. His mother devotes her life to her son, over-compensating for the loss of the father and suffocating Pink with her love.

He attends schools that subjugate the children rather than educating them. He is exposed to teachers who chastise and suppress children, seeking to free their own miserable frustrations. His response to these alienating experiences is to slowly build a defensive 'wall' around his feelings, to shelter him from further hurt. Pink marries his childhood sweetheart because she is conveniently available.

The boy has grown up and become a Rock and Roll performer, part of a band, attracted by the 'power and fame' which help to insulate him against his nagging feelings of separation, not only from his wife and friends, but also from himself. This is a life of diminishing returns. Like an addict with his junk, Pink needs bigger and bigger fixes of applause.

But it's never enough. The endless separations build the wall still higher between Pink and his wife, until the inevitable happens – while he is away on tour, she falls in love with another man. The final brick in Pink's wall.

Pink locks himself in his room with a handful of pills and a groupie. He destroys the furniture and frightens the girl away. Alone now, drugged and with only the TV for company, he retreats more and more into himself, the 'wall' is now complete. Totally withdrawn from the real world, his imagination wanders into the further extremities of his nightmare, his worst fears, his probable madness.

He imagines himself as an unfeeling demagogue, for whom all that is left is the exercise of power over his unthinking, uncaring audience. His manager, concerned as always about the forthcoming show, breaks into the hotel room and a doctor revives Pink enough to get him out of the hotel and into the limousine. But Pink has long gone. He hallucinates wildly as the real world vanishes, and he conjures up an evil spectacular, a Rock and roll Nuremburg with himself as its leader: the cumulation of the odious excess of his own world and the world around him.

It is all too much for the core of human feeling, and he rebels. STOP! His internal self-trial follows, as the witnesses of his past life, the very people who have contributed to the building of the wall, come forward to testify against him. The judgement is that he must 'tear down the wall' before his isolation leads him into the moral decay of his nightmares.

Over Victoria Falls in a Barrel

Six months after the release of 'The Wall' double album, allegedly produced for $700,000, the live show was' premièred at the Los Angeles Sports Arena from February 7 to 11 1980. As everyone knows by now, the climax was the construction of a wall of 420 cardboard 'bricks' across the arena, 160ft long and 30ft high, which was destroyed after the intermission. The first night was delayed when fireworks set light to overhead drapes during the first half and everyone had to wait for the show to go on while the fire brigade extinguished the flames.

Gerald Scarfe, responsible for the entire 'Wall' visual look, says: 'Roger saw right at the beginning that "The Wall" could be an album, a show and a film. Roger played me the raw tapes of his score and we began to discuss it as a movie.

'I had already done some work with the Floyd, and after a while it became clear that we should try to do "The Wall" on stage before attempting anything else. It was immensely complicated, with huge inflatables which I built hovering over the group and a vast wall of cardboard bricks which spanned the auditorium at the climax of the piece. Despite the complications it always went off like clockwork wherever it was performed. And the interesting thing was that the audience simply sat there, drinking in the spectacle.'

The band were tax exiles, being unable to pay their 83 per cent of earnings to H.M. Inland Revenue because of the Norton Warburg crash, so until they could return to England on April 15 they lived at the Tropicana Motor Hotel on Santa Monica Boulevard. The British concerts were planned for the Milton Keynes open-air arena (capacity 35,000), but then shifted to the more familiar (and smaller) venue of Earls Court for a week from August 4.

It was Bob Mercer of EMI who put Roger Waters in touch with director Alan Parker ('Midnight Express', 'Fame'), but because Parker was involved in making 'Shoot the Moon', it was agreed that Parker's director of photography, Michael Seresin, should co-direct alongside Scarfe. Scarfe also happens to be married to Jane Asher, the sister of ex-pop star and now management heavy, Peter Asher, who had promoted the Floyd concerts in the Sixties, and handled the Waters '84 tour.

During the German leg of the 'Wall' concerts, Seresin and Parker flew to see them in Dortmund. Parker's recollections give a better picture of them than any of the critical notices that appeared in the music press at the time: 'It was impossible not to be impressed by the power of the proceedings. The concert was Rock Theatre on the grandest scale. Probably more grandiose and ambitious than it had ever been. The sound was awesome, the Floyd musically precise and Roger's primal scream, the fears of madness, oppression and alienation cutting through the giant theatricals. You couldn't fail to be astonished by the sheer scale of the mechanical undertaking and the colossal engineering problems that had been overcome to present it.

'Coming from the slow, almost archaic film process, to see *everything* – every sound fader pushed correctly, every hoist, every light, every cue hit on time, was wonderfully impressive. The high points for me were the guitar solo in "Comfortably Numb" that Dave Gilmour performed precariously perched on top of the wall, back lit, his weird surreal three-dimensional shadow bleeding across the faces of the 10,000-plus audience. Also I had a chance to see Gerry Scarfe's animation for the first time. The flowers making love I thought were brilliant, and when the marching hammers of oppression burst across the mammoth screen formed by the wall, in tryptych, with three projectors synchronised together with the live show sound, it was a theatrical sensation I knew would be difficult to contain within the confines of a regular screen. Anamorphic Panavision and Dolby sound suddenly looked pathetic by comparison.

'Backstage it was just as impressive – no cliché rock and roll parties, but an ultra-cool and professional atmosphere, not entirely relaxed, a little edgy in fact, but people with a job to do, that happened to do with being rock and roll stars.

'Also of note was how everything was dominated by Roger's almost demonic control of the proceedings.

'Now you could have put ten cameras on that, cut it together very quickly and we would have had a film we could then sell to cable and video. We decided not to do that and instead make a regular feature film with a life of its own.'

The film business was less enthusiastic. Live concert movies have never been great box office, and Parker recalled, 'as I would describe the unusual nature of the film to the film moguls – major and minor – a fragmented piece with no conventional dialogue to progress the narrative, with music as its main driving force, they would stare back at me with total incredulity.

'It could have been a 100 per cent British thing. The album was British, the group British and we're British. EMI had a chance to commit. I was asked to go round and talk to the EMI field force and tell them what kind of film it was. Alan Marshall (Parker's producer) and I did our usual "tap dancing" routine, but then we were handed the usual EMI phrase, "This is something we can't go with right now". Yet another opportunity missed.' In the end, David Begelman of MGM took up the offer, with the Floyd themselves contributing 12 million dollars of the cost.

The original idea had been to use a Floyd concert as a unifying factor, and accordingly Earls Court was booked for a re-run of the 'Wall' shows for five days from June 13 1981.

'The shooting was a total disaster,' says Parker. 'Michael and Gerry didn't quite jel as directors and I myself, quite useless as an impotent director masquerading as a not-too-helpful producer, began chain-smoking for the first time in my life. From the start, the dilemma was always compromising the theatrics of the show for the needs of the film. The show, better organized and ticking along like a precision-made behemoth, couldn't be spoiled by film crews, not ever sure of what they were supposed to be doing.

'The fast Panavision lenses, needed for the low light levels, had no resolution, so the rushes looked like they'd been shot through soup. A Louma crane shot that scaled the wall to reveal the thousands in the crowd as Roger sang "Hey You" never got its complicated moves right – and with five live shows it only had five chances, all muffed. For myself, I'd shaken David Begelman's hand, and was beginning to think I might let him down. As I nervously walked back and forth during the show, watching the performance from a dozen different vantage points,

124

inhaling the contents of three packs of cigarettes or sitting alone backstage in the peculiar astroturfed Floyd inner sanctum, it was obvious that it couldn't go on like this. Either we abandoned the film or I had to come out of the producer's closet and start directing proper. The Floyd, who were footing the bills themselves at this point, had come to the same conclusions.'

Another disaster as the attempt to create an electronically-controlled teacher robot, to bring to life Gerald Scarfe's drawing, but though a lot of money and time was put into it, it tended to overpower the settings. 'Indeed,' says Parker, 'hardly any of the theatrical devices survived as the reality and surreality of our film took over.'

On Monday September 7, 1981, shooting began in earnest under Parker's personal direction at the East Molesey home of a retired admiral, which was to be the home of young Pink. While they were shooting inside, an exterior crew were trying to shoot the sequence where a dove is stalked by a cat, and flies into the sky – after which it runs into the animated sequence where it is transformed into a war eagle. They lost 50 doves and 20 pigeons and got 'a few fuzzy frames of usable fluttering wings'.

The playground sequence was shot in Bermondsey, the rugby field sequence on Epsom Downs at 5.30am, with specially erected rugger posts, the 'Los Angeles Arena' exteriors outside Wembley, and the Anzio bridgehead sequence at Burnham Beaches, Barnstaple. The 200 'soldiers' recruited from the local labour exchange demanded extra money when they found they'd have to share the trenches with live rats. The two model Stuka divebombers didn't survive the shoot: one nosedived into the sand before any footage had been shot and the other disintegrated in mid-air after it had done its duty by the director.

The hotel interiors were shot in Pinewood, using the long special effects tunnel for the opening sequence in the hotel corridor, with a special Samcine inclining prism on the Panaflex camera for a really low carpet-level shot. The hotel room, with computerized backdrop representing the lights of Los Angeles, plus penthouse swimming pool, holding 70 tons of water, was constructed on the large 'D' stage at Pinewood.

Playing Pink, Bob Geldof hurt himself quite a bit during the room-smashing sequence, which was shot by John Stanier, a man Parker says has 'ballet dancer's feet and bricklayers's shoulders', using a hand-held camera. The slow-motion falling of a drop of blood during the unpleasant 'Don't Leave Me Now' eyebrow-shaving sequence had been shot by Oxford Scientific Films, who usually apply their expertise to recording the sexual habits of insects. 'At one time,' recalled Parker, 'I had thought of using the sexual mores and violence in the insect world as metaphors in our story but it was soon abandoned – anyway, the rate these diligent scientists work, we would still be finishing the film.'

Oxford also did the extreme close-up panning from Pink's Mickey Mouse watch up his arm to end on his eye, using a specially-developed electronically-controlled gadget.

Parker admits to nicking quite a few ideas from the pioneer Frenchman, Abel Gance, whose epic silent movie, 'Napoleon', had just been resurrected and performed in London with a newly-composed live score by Carl Davis: like suspending the camera on a pendulum to shoot Geldof thrashing around in the blood-stained pool.

The huge wall was built at Pinewood for the 'Goodbye Cruel World', 'Is There Anybody There?' and 'Hey You' sequences, and then blown down with an air cannon, previously used in a James Bond movie.

It was the location scenes of youthful violence which caused many of the greatest problems in crowd control. They'd originally intended to stage the 'rock Nuremberg' in a specially constructed set, but eventually they settled for the New Horticultural Hall, London, where 380 skinheads, a choir of 24, a brass band of 21, six mothers with babies and 24 guards assembled under the control of assistant diretor Ray Corbett, who lost his voice shouting orders over the next couple of days.

'The toughest section of the skinhead crowd,' said Parker, 'were a group called the Tilbury Skins from South East London. We'd partially defused the threat of real violence by promoting this group to a more prestigious position in the film. They were to play Pink's "Hammer Guard", and we were going to use this bunch of amiable looneys as the kernel of the recreated violence that was to follow. Our stunt co-ordinator had been working with them for a month previously at Pinewood, showing them the rudiments of film stunting, the ability to punch someone without the need for breaking their jaw, and we'd arrived at a sort of disciplined logic to their behaviour.

'Well, sort of. I remember the crowd reactions as Bob first made the entry for "In the Flesh II", and then proceeded to sing the odious lyrics – the sheer spectacle of the proceedings was very seductive and I can remember my fears of people taking it too seriously – and the niggling feeling always that we should make it quite clear to the film audience that what they were watching was created: the exercise of power by an inflated, demented persona over a mindless audience . . .

'The most alarming feeling was in the pub at lunchtime, when our jackbooted guards in full uniform walked in and ordered their pints. The local residents, unaware that it was a film, weren't sure what to make of it. For them the reality of this impending evil was too close to home.' Gerald Scarfe had created the uniforms and the 'crossed hammers' insignia that were the livery of Pink's followers in such a realistic manner that he wondered if he might have manufactured a Frankenstein's monster.

'I invented a skinhead militia called the Hammer Guard,' he said. 'Their insignia is two crossed hammers and my worst moment in the entire film was when one skinhead turned up with his hair shaved into the hammer design. I have nightmares about meeting people in the street who've taken up the Hammer Look. Of course, we were not endorsing violence. But what the film says is that by creating a wall between people it is entirely possible – you could say inevitable – that violence will occur. Somehow the wall has to be broken down.'

For 'Run Like Hell', choreographer Gillian Gregory had coached the Hammer-adorned skins in a Nazi disco routine in batches of 100 at a time to get them something approaching the Busby Berkeley-like precision she was seeking. 'I remember my feelings as the assembled skinheads dutifully performed their fascist "dance" for the first time to the playback tapes,' said Parker, 'complete with choreographed sieg heils, donning their pink masks and so wiping out their personalities and taking away their individuality as they became anonymous, acting as one in an unthinking, programmed, mechanical mass. At the end of the piece, on stage, Bob goaded them into action with his crossed arms "hammer" salute. This they followed with a zombie-like precision, perfected on the terraces of West Ham and Millwall.'

West Ham, one of the strongholds of the Nazi National Front among working class football hooligans, uses the hammer as its symbol.

The words in the shooting script merely read 'we cut to the broader issues', but Scarfe's nightmare seemed to be about to come true when the time came to take the riot scenes in a disused gasworks at Becton on the 57th day of shooting. The callsheet read: 150 rioters and police, stunts, police riot equipment, two police vans, police cars, FX fire, smoke and explosions, tear gas guns. The crew had to work ankle deep in wet coal dust, so they demanded dirty money – and got it.

'The riot footage was an improvized affair that developed through the night,' reported Parker. 'The only image I'd preconceived was the "wall" of riot police, their shields glinting in the light, behind them a second wall of flames.

'As the night drew on and the skinheads and "police" clashed for the dozenth time, tempers were rising. The skinheads had found it difficult to grasp that these were actors *dressed* as policemen and that we were creating a *film* riot, not a real one. But, however many times we reminded them, the fighting always seemed to continue long after I had yelled out "Cut!" They'd also tried to film some faked up football violence at Watford ground, recreating a stabbing incident that had actually happened at a European Cup match a short time before, but the

127

resultant footage didn't stand comparison with the real thing seen by millions of viewers on their TV screens, so most of it was junked. A short segment can be seen in the 'Waiting for the Worms' sequence, if you look carefully.

The Tilbury skins, 'who couldn't believe their luck', were also given the task of smashing up a 'Brixton' cafe (actually constructed behind King's Cross Station in North London) for the 'Run Like Hell' sequence, which Parker describes as 'probably the ugliest I'd ever directed'.

'The rape scene was the most repugnant of all, and any amount of jokes didn't detract from the unpleasant vicarious involvement you have as film makers. On the final cut we kept the scene down to a minimum, as some of the shots were a little too much for us to take in rushes, let alone an audience in a cinema.'

The Becton gasworks were also used for the scenes where the kids revolt and destroy their school. The sequence began in the studio, with actors destroying the actual sets – an idea that Parker may have got from the 'Marat-Sade' movie, where the Royal Shakespeare actors and actresses were encouraged to have a farewell orgy after filming had supposedly finished. The cameras were in fact still rolling, and the resulting footage was much more effective than the previous, staged take.

Under the watchful eyes of the local fire brigade, the film's Special FX department razed the derelict gasworks. 'The result is one of the scarier moments in the film, and one which we hope people won't misinterpret,' said Parker afterwards. 'We were keen that the whole message should be viewed as a murky surreal daydream in young Pink's mind, as he is bullied by the teacher for writing poetry.'

Bob Geldof was less worried. 'Every kid has thoughts of how delicious it would be to burn down school – just as adults dream of burning down their offices.'

After shooting was completed, Parker and his editors had 16 weeks to assemble the 350,000 feet of film (playing time 60 hours) into the final 99-minute print, cutting together the 977 separate shots in the script – editor Gerry Hambling made nearly 5,500 cuts to fit it all together. It was then that the difficulties between Waters and Parker, never far below the surface, began to explode like the sleeping volcanoes they'd been all along. When he first took over the directing, Parker had stipulated that Roger 'stepped back a bit to give me some air so that I could clarify my own vision of the piece', and Roger had conveniently taken six weeks' holiday while Parker mulled it over.

Describing this period in an interview, Parker made the remark which still seems to rankle with Waters: 'I took the blueprint of our script (just 39 pages) and began to formulate in my mind the images that would accompany the music to tell our story.' Roger has refused to comment on his problems in collaborating with Alan Parker, still less to issue any kind of rebuttal of what the director has said in countless interviews around the world, and he is also generous in his praise for Parker's work in bringing the job in within budget, and on time, despite the immense logistical problems.

'The man's a very good technician,' he said to me. 'He really is. And by God he gets things done. He shot the thing in however long it was, six weeks or something.

'If I knew what I know now – the main thing I've learned about films is that when you're making them, first of all I looked at the rushes every day, almost every day, and then slowly as you go through the editing you assemble stuff and then you see it a reel at a time, generally speaking, and then you may put one or two reels together or three – you tend not to look at the whole thing together.

'The dubbing was done one reel at a time. And what may look terrific as one reel is not necessarily good in the context of the whole film – reel five to me looked great but it may not be good between reel four and reel six.

'My main criticism of the film is that there aren't any dull moments, and consequently every bit of it become dull. D'you follow what I'm saying?'

'You're talking about dynamics.'

'Yeah, it's not dynamic. It goes *chchchch*, then it goes *khkhkhkh*, for 90 minutes. Knowing what I know now I would not have allowed that to happen. I didn't see it happening.

'I think you cannot make a good film if every minute of it looks good on its own. I think that's the nature of things. You've got to have, you know, periods that look like nothing, until they're in context.

'Parker has a terrible fear of boring his audience. People in retrospect have said that you get that from people who've worked for years and years on commercials, because that's the whole thing, get the bloody audience gripped. It's like making the three-minute single, you know. It's like people would listen to my stuff in the old days and think: That's no good, you don't get the hook in the first 15 seconds. Forget it!

'Well it's a bit like the same thing with making commercials, you've got to get them and then hold them for 20 seconds. They get terrified, consequently their films are like that the whole time, one thing after another after another and it actually makes it more difficult to become involved with the thing rather than less difficult.'

The personality problems had begun to surface between the two men when they worked together with Scarfe on the script. 'For Roger it was never a case of writing a script,' Parker recalled, 'it was about delving into his psyche to find personal truths whereas I was more interested in cinematic action. Indeed, if I veered too far he would say: "But that's not how it happened". Gerry would quietly and unemotionally preside over these stormy "special brew" days between Roger and myself, and when we left, would draw up the day's thoughts into a wonderful giant storyboard that grew larger and larger, gradually spreading across the walls of his studio.'

I hate to call anyone a liar, but I doubt the detail of this recollection. The story line of 'The Wall' is only partly autobiographical – the character of the mother is totally at odds with Roger's real mother, for instance – and it seems to me Roger would probably have been more anxious to convey the nitty gritty reality of what rock and roll is like, rather than to delve into his own psyche. All legends to the contrary, Roger Waters is a balanced and professional man, in the most practical sense of the word. He can get very emotional, and he's very vulnerable, but he has the power – the gift of all artists – to combine the management of the concrete realities of his life with the nurturing of his artistic *daemon*, using his very vulnerability as a spark from which he lights the fire of his creativity.

However, there were undoubtedly rows, though Parker describes them as 'never more than arm wrestling'.

'We collided one day in the dubbing theatre,' he recalled, 'both spouting venom, like the judge in the animation. Frankly, our problems were never really about the film, but about ego and creative authorship. I think he was fearful that I wouldn't let him back in, and I was just as paranoid about the cut being tampered with or improved to death. Fortunately, Gerry Hambling was smarter than both of us, and continued to astound us with brilliant editing.'

Scarfe's view of the temperamental clashes was more resigned. 'You could say that the collaborative process has been filled with angst,' he said. 'But possibly out of that will come something rather special. After all, we're only an artist, a musician and a film maker. I wonder if Picasso and Stravinsky would ever have had these problems?'

The film was to be previewed at Cannes, where eventually it secured an out-of-competition prize, and engineer James Guthrie was working against time in Pinewood's Theatre 2 dubbing suite, cramming in three 24-track tape decks and the associated console so that he could copy direct from the original master tapes on to the film. This was to avoid the loss of quality that is usual with the many generations of sound copying employed in normal film recording. They also had to record some new music, 'When the Tigers Broke Free', and new versions of 'Mother', 'In the Flesh II', 'Outside the Wall' (with silver band), and

'Bring the Boys Back Home' (with full orchestra and Welsh choir). They also recorded a specially composed prelude which never found its way on to the film soundtrack.

That still left the animations to edit. Gerry Scarfe had worked with 50 artists over three years to produce a total of 14,000 individual hand-coloured drawings for the 15 or so minutes of animation in the film. Scarfe had decided not to use the computerised techniques familiar to kids who watch the 'Flintstones' and their TV ilk, because they weren't natural enough. 'They had to be drawn by hand because, up to now, that's the only satisfactory way to draw organic movement. Even if you had a computer suitably programmed, the drawings would still have a stylised quality.' Scarfe had also had to adapt his style, 'from Sunday Times scratchy-pen approach to something that could be copied by other artists'. 'The reason that Disney drew the way he did was because everyone could draw like Disney, at least everyone who could draw,' he pointed out. 'So to do this I had to explore other areas of my work, which was very exciting.'

The sort of transition from live action to animation, including sets built to false perspective, which made the film so effective when seen finally, was described by director of photography Peter Biziou: 'The camera pulls back from a medium closeup of Pink in his armchair to a very wide angle and we discover either the room is very large or he's very small. Then the shadow of his wife appears on the wall. She is walking towards him and growing in size and very smoothly her form becomes Gerald Scarfe's animation which continues growing into a gross figure that is persecuting Pink. Brian Morris' (production designer) 'had to build a very large room and cheat the perspective. We kept Pink and all the furniture the same normal size so that as the camera pulls back you are given the impression that he's totally alienated in this very, very large room.'

When the film opened, on July 14 1982, it had cost £7 million. It broke box-office records at the Empire Leicester Square, where it took £49,161 the first week. The critics were less impressed, running through the usual depleted vocabulary or words like 'depressing', 'shallow', 'self-indulgent', and 'bleak'. One of the more balanced (though he didn't like it much) was Derek Malcolm in the Guardian, who wrote: '. . . if Parker's masterstrokes sometimes alienate rather than proving very much about alienation, his smaller visions, amply detailed by the camera, seem remarkably real. And the concert that is really the film's finale, the natural summation of Pink's neurosis, is as powerfully filmed as anything in "Tommy", the other British success in this area.

'Above all, Parker's visual synthesis with the music, much aided by

131

Scarfe's rip-roaring visions of doom and destruction which turn light into darkness at the flick of a pen rather than a switch, is almost perfect. He has got rhythm all right, and if you want to know how to cut a film to it, watch this one. It is a very carefully constructed shambles, as it was intended to be – a chaotic pointer to chaotic times, hyped up beyond the point of no return, so that you finally accept almost every enormity is possible.

'The brilliance, however, is never quite enough, and only in sections of the film is the depth of focus as impressive as the width. But since that's precisely what one feels about Pink Floyd, one can hardly blame the film-maker for that.'

According to Cinefantastique magazine (a US glossy, despite its Frenchified name), Roger Waters had meant the concert sequence Malcolm liked so much to be even more violent; more like 'a punch in the face'. 'In the original script,' it said, 'during the concert number ("In the Flesh"), the rock audience was to have been blown up, gorily destroyed, while enjoying and applauding every minute of it, even as they died.'

Before shooting began, Parker told his crew it would be a bit like Livingstone going up the Zambesi. After it was finished, he declared it had been more like going over Victoria Falls in a barrel.

The Album and the Movie

Though there are certain obvious differences between 'The Wall' music as originally conceived for the album and the way it is heard in the movie, much of it is identical. Roger Waters even controlled the faders in the dubbing suite for the film. There is also, as we have seen, one new song, 'When the Tigers Broke Free', and the new versions of 'Mother', 'In the Flesh Part II', 'Outside the Wall', and 'Bring the Boys Back Home', as well as the inclusion of the old Vera Lynn song, 'The Little Boy That Santa Claus Forgot', at the very beginning.

The running order is also different.

ALBUM	MOVIE
	The Little Boy That Santa Claus Forgot
	When the Tigers Broke Free, Part 1
In the Flesh?	In the Flesh
The Thin Ice	The Thin Ice
Another Brick in the Wall, Part 1	Another Brick in the Wall, Part 1
	When the Tigers Broke Free, Part 2

	Goodbye Blue Sky
The Happiest Days of Our Lives	The Happiest Days of Our Lives
Another Brick in the Wall, Part 2	Another Brick in the Wall, Part 2
Mother	Mother
Goodbye Blue Sky	
Empty Spaces	Empty Spaces
Young Lust	Young Lust
One of My Turns	One of My Turns
Don't Leave Me Now	Don't Leave Me Now
Another Brick in the Wall, Part 3	Another Brick in the Wall, Part 3
Goodbye, Cruel World	Goodbye, Cruel World
Hey You	
Is There Anybody Out There?	Is There Anybody Out There?
Nobody Home	Nobody Home
Vera	Vera
Bring the Boys Back Home	Bring the Boys Back Home
Comfortably Numb	Comfortably Numb
The Show Must Go On	
In the Flesh	In the Flesh
Run Like Hell	Run Like Hell
Waiting for the Worms	Waiting for the Worms
Stop	Stop
The Trial	The Trial
Outside the Wall	Outside the Wall

All alone, or in twos,
The ones who really love you
Walk up and down outside the wall.
Some hand in hand.
Some gathering together in bands.
The bleeding hearts and the artists
Make their stand.
And when they've given you their all,
Some stagger and fall, after all it's not easy
Banging your heart against some mad bugger's Wall.

Extracts from an interview with
Roger Waters, September 22 1982

DALLAS: How much of Pink is in you, or how much of you is in Pink?

WATERS: My father was killed in the war, at Anzio. I did find the scroll and the uniform in a drawer one day. The playground stuff, I don't remember that, that's something that I wrote just to keep the scene going, that might have to do with the character.

DALLAS: Was your childhood as unhappy as 'The Wall' seems to suggest?

WATERS: No.
Why does 'The Wall' seem to suggest a very unhappy childhood? Because of the school, you mean? And being rejected in the playground by the man?

DALLAS: And also his relationship with his mother, which . . .

WATERS: No, my relationship with my mother wasn't like that. In fact the mother is one of the bad areas of characterisation in the film, I think. She's full of contradictions, that character, really. Not very well drawn. I think that may have something to do with the fact that I didn't draw very much on my own experience for that area. I mean I did find a dying rat on the rugby field and take it home and try to look after it, and my own mother did make me put in the garage, but not like that. She wasn't a crazy, over-weight, hysterical woman. I think that's a very crude portrayal of that response. It's a cliche . . . it's not the way . . . I think it's wrong.

DALLAS: Is she still alive?

WATERS: My mother? Yeah.

DALLAS: Have you explained this to her?

WATERS: Oh yeah, yeah. When the record came out – she hasn't seen the film yet, in fact I'm going to take her to see it in a couple of weeks when she comes up to town – when the record came out, I talked to her about it, and warned her what it was about.

DALLAS: What about specific incidents, like smashing up the hotel room?

WATERS: No, I've never done that. Again, no I've never done any of that, but again, that's something borrowed from other people's experience.

DALLAS: I also suspect that not only was your childhood not as unhappy as the album and the film suggests but slightly more privileged. I think you come from a slightly sort of better social background than that, don't you?

WATERS: Um, well we never find out in the film what she does, do we? That's another thing. You never find out who they are, really. It's a perfectly nice house that they're living in and he's very well dressed in his little mac and his . . .

But that's the other thing about that bit of the film: one was never quite sure where it was or who they were or what the background was, in fact, or I wasn't, watching it. It skimmed over the surface rather of all that.

My mother was a school-teacher, in a university town, in Cambridge. I mean, Cambridge was a very nice place to live.

I had a fantastic time. I didn't like school, I didn't like my grammar school. I hated it. But I enjoyed life at my primary school, a lot. I actually went to a very good primary school. It was just that immediate postwar period where enormous strides were made in primary education in this country, where it started to be focussed far less about, you know, 'sit still, shut up, and learn to read and write' and more about centres of interest and projects about things and . . .

But my grammar school was pretty dreadful.

DALLAS: One of the things that struck me is that a lot of the kids who go to see it won't ever have experienced being treated that way in the classroom.

WATERS: Mind you, I think quite a lot of people who are going to see the film aren't kids, in fact.

The idea behind all that really was to suggest that as far as he was concerned, the character, that it may only take one isolated incident, with one bad teacher, to affect the way the person responds to people maybe for the rest of his life. I believe that.

I can remember being really very badly upset, even when I was quite old, by people suddenly giving vent to their personal frustrations at my expense. But it is a bit confused, that area.

DALLAS: So the teacher is probably more modelled on your real-life experience than your mother.

WATERS: Yes, oh yes. Without question.

DALLAS: I mean, is there a teacher in your mind, when you . . .?

WATERS: Not one specific one, but we had a number. We had some good teachers as well, but we had a fair number who were serving their time and who were extremely bitter about all

135

sorts of different things and who as I say were so frustrated and bitter about their lives that they treated the kids at school abominably.

And they would often pick on the weak ones as well and make their lives a misery for them.

It was a war, it was a real war with lots of them. And a real battle, and sometimes the battle was won by the kids and I can remember teachers at my grammar school having nervous breakdowns.

One guy one afternoon just went and got on the train. Nobody knew. He was found wandering about in the early hours of next morning a hundred miles away, which seemed incredibly funny at the time.

Because of the way we felt and the fact that we felt it was a battle, in fact, we behaved in the same way. We followed their example. The nasty sarcastic ones that picked on the weak kids, that affected us to the extent that we picked on the weak teachers.

But I'm sure, in fact I know, there are all kinds of troubles in schools all over the country, but I think the atmosphere has changed to a certain extent. I don't think they attempt that absolute exercise of power in the same way that they did when I was at school.

The thing is that if I'm writing a song something like that, it's not like conducting a reasoned argument or writing an essay or conducting a debate or something, it's just about expressing my own particular, ultimately, inevitably, biassed feelings, and getting them out in a song, if I can, and if people pick up on them, that's good. But I wouldn't claim, you know, that the picture that Scarfe and myself between us painted of this character's schooldays, I wouldn't claim it was not a caricature. It is a caricature.

We weren't trying to remake 'Kes', which was beautiful and poetic and real, apparently. One had a great feeling that those situations were real. 'The Wall' is a very stylized work, and it is a work of satire and caricature.

DALLAS: And are you also satirized and caricatured in it?

WATERS: M'm, yes. I mean the character is. Because what happens is that the character recognizes, within himself, a lust for power and a lack of caring for other people's feelings and other people's needs, which he then projects into a fantasy of himself as a kind of fascist demagogue.

I'm not sure if that's satire, but it's an attack on parts

of myself that I disapprove of, a sort of exercise in self-flagellation, I suppose. No, that's wrong, that's the wrong image.

The film gets so odd at that point, halfway through, the way that the character's examination of himself is portrayed – because that's what it is – that I don't know what I'd call it.

DALLAS: I can think of a lot of people it's more obviously like, rock stars, who are in fact fascist demagogues, in the way they behave on stage, their relationship with the audience.

WATERS: Well, clearly, it's pointing to all that, and pointing at them. Mind you, nobody seems to have spotted that, really. And the whole thing about the relationship between musicians and their audiences is something . . . in the very first draft of a screenplay that I wrote, that area was dealt with more adequately, more deeply. There was more screen time devoted to it.

DALLAS: Do you regret that change of emphasis?

WATERS: Yes, partially. I think there's a bit too much kind of wandering up and down misty railway embankments and things. I think all that childhood stuff got a bit drawn-out in the end and I think the first 20 minutes is pretty slow, really. And, yeah, I regret that that feeling of mine isn't expressed more strongly in it. Some of it is expressed as strongly as I could have hoped for, really, you know the kind of self-destructive instincts of the whoopers and hollerers . . .

DALLAS: In the audience?

WATERS: Yeah. That kind of crazed rush into an empty auditorium is something that I used to watch from time to time in big, big places like the Cow Palace in San Francisco, that crazed rush to the front of the stage, to stand crushed against the barriers for hour after hour after hour.

DALLAS: The cross-cutting in the movie, with the Anzio landings, don't you think that's a little far-fetched?

WATERS: Not really, no. I don't. Because there seems to me to be something . . . well, it's strange, because it's not a direct parallel. Clearly, the motivation behind people jumping off DUKWs and running up beaches in Anzio is that they've been bloody well ordered to do it, you know. And they thought, and they were probably right in thinking, they were fighting a war that needed to be fought.

Whereas the motivation for the kind of involvement in

137

rock shows that I'm pointing at is a masochism. It's something I don't understand. I do not understand that thing of people going to rock shows and apparently the more painful it is the better they like it.

There are lots of shows where the sound is just so awful and so loud that it's painful. And it becomes a kind of religious exercise almost, it seems to me. It's a bit like being a whirling dervish or something, you achieve ecstasy through continual repetition of some simple movement.

Maybe that's what it is. Maybe it's a response to a lack of religious involvement. It's a bit like walking on hot coals or something. Certainly you see people sometimes at shows where they've gone to be in the presence of their Gods and whatever happens, really, they're going to bloody well make all the right responses in all the right places, come hell or high water.

So that is something that I found depressing in rock 'n' roll and that's what I found depressing in the tour we did in '77, just that it seemed to me to not be anything about musicians and audiences enjoying being in each other's company – just one group of people performing and the others listening or watching or whatever – but a series of situations where the response was conditioned and automatic and where all it was about was money, or very, very little else.

I mean I can say this because I believe it, on a tour like the Stones' last tour, this world-wide tour that they've done, the money is so much more important than anything else that it completely overshadows, as far as I can see anyway, anything else that's going on. It has become absolutely the central issue in that situation.

And the media picks up on it, everybody picks up on it. That's all the media are interested in, is how much money they made, how many T-shirts they sold.

DALLAS: Isn't that partly because what the Stones are doing musically, at the moment, is not very interesting, so that's all there is to write about?

WATERS: I don't know, that may be so. That may be so, yeah.

But you know, the Stones' music has never been very *interesting*, with a capital I. You know. It's been fucking good, it's been great.

When I was a kid . . . (laughs)

138

DALLAS: How old are you now, Roger?

WATERS: 39.

When I was a kid, they were g-r-eat! I was an incredible Stones fan. I still am, actually. I still think some of the stuff that they do is really good. I just think their shows are a joke, all those fucking people crammed into those big stadiums, I think they're just as much of a joke for them as they were for us.

DALLAS: You use the past tense. Does that mean you think that your later shows aren't a joke?

WATERS: Yeah. Well it's only 'The Wall'. That's all we've done since then. We did those, I thought, under much more controlled conditions, i.e. 15 thousand people instead of 80 thousand people. All that makes a hell of a difference. You can cater to 15 thousand people, with the technology that's available now. If you take it seriously enough and get the right people in to help an spend enough of *their* money on it, because it's the punters' money for God's sake. So if you spend enough of it on sound systems and on what you do, then you can at least take care of the technical aspects of the thing and provide a decent return for whatever it is that they have to pay, and still do something that you find interesting yourself, obviously. I thought, 'The Wall' shows were . . . I know they were very expensive, they were eight quid or something, the tickets were, but that's how much they cost. That's what it cost. You could make out a case for saying well, people would rather have paid two quid and not have any of that show, well, that may be true, but that was what I was interested in doing. It was a gamble, obviously.

DALLAS: Because a lot of the time in 'The Wall', people thought they were listening to you and they weren't, were they? They were listening to the surrogate musicians.

WATERS: Well at the beginning, yeah, at the very begining. Actually, the idea was that they were, clearly they were meant to be what we became, i.e. at that juncture Pink was like a gestalt figure, the whole band turned into this kind of Nazi apparition towards the end of the thing, and that was really a kind of theatrical shock tactic, because people would assume that it was us and ask 'Why are they dressed in those weird clothes? What's going on?' And wonder about things.

And then suddenly realise that it wasn't actually us. I

139

just wanted to create a sort of confused atmosphere at the beginning so that people could start to sort it out slowly as the show went on. It may be that it was too confusing, but what I liked about doing 'The Wall' and why it was different from touring in '77 which we did with 'Animals' and 'Wish You Were Here', which were also fairly rigidly constructed pieces, was that in 'The Wall' we provided the audience with enough stuff so that it was almost impossible not to be involved in it, if you were in the audience, *I* think. And that was what the intention was, really, to do a rock show which didn't have to rely necessarily on the feeling of being in the presence of divine beings, or getting some contact-high from being close to power and wealth and fame . . .

DALLAS: You don't think that the very construction of it in fact made that even more so? Here's a guy who's so big that he can afford to put a wall between him and the audience?

WATERS: Well, that's the point it was making. But I mean it was making the point, yeah, about us as much as about other bands, except it was something that I personally had become very aware of. So if you like I was really, at that point, sharing my awareness of the situation with other people. I know a hell of a lot of people picked up on it. I'm sure there were a hell of a lot of people who didn't, who came to the show and went away thinking 'What the fuck was all that about?'. And aren't interested, anyway. There's no reason why everybody should be interested in the same things I am, at all.

DALLAS: I found it rather oppressive. I was quite pleased I didn't actually have to review it because I did not have a good time.

WATERS: Really?

DALLAS: I felt as if I'd been attacked, not a personal attack, like 'You, yer bastard', but just that I'd been under psychic attack.

WATERS: Well, you had, I suppose. You had. It wasn't, you know, it wasn't meant to be a sort of wonderful, 'God isn't it wonderful, here we are all together let's have a good time' concert, that's obviously not what it was about.

And clearly the film isn't, either. You don't go to the film and come away thinking 'Christ, that was wonderful'.

DALLAS: But both the show and the film end on an up-note.

WATERS: Yes. That's true. That final song is saying, 'Right, well that was it, you've seen it now. That's the best we can do, really. And that wasn't actually us. This is us. That was us performing a piece of theatre about the things that it was about and we do like you really.' I mean we do need that human contact, that's just making a little bit of human contact at the end of the show.

The backwards and forwards about how to end that show, the different kind of things that we went through!

I mean originally, in the very, very first version of it, the plan was just to build the wall and leave it. But that was too tough, really, too kind of alienating, and didn't feel right at the time.

We didn't not do that because of the worry about how people would respond. We didn't do that because it was too tough, it was too 'Fuck you', which wasn't the intention at all.

Anyway, it's not something that I'd care to do again, but it's something that I'm glad to have been part of.

DALLAS: That means we're not going to see 'The Wall' live again?

WATERS: I wouldn't have thought so, no. I can't imagine that, the aggravation of getting it together. You never know. We won't be certain about that for another few years when one will know that everything has rotted and all the machinery is rusty. If you haven't seen it again in the next five years then you'll know you're not going to, because everything will have been stolen or rusted away, the cardboard will all be soggy.

DALLAS: The film ending is also upbeat, but it seems to be saying something different but equally in contrast with the alienation of the earlier part.

WATERS: M'm. (pause) Yeah. What do you think it's saying?

DALLAS: It seems to me – I'll answer your question this way – that the movie is much more politically orientated. It's not merely that it uses images of rioting, but I mean that final image, kids playing . .

WATERS: Yeah, absolutely, yeah. That final image, if it's saying anything at all, it's suggesting that when we're born, we don't like Molotov cocktails, and that we learn to like them as we grow older. We learn to want to burn stuff and break things. But then we're that age . . . you know, children don't like the smell of petrol and they don't like the taste of whisky. These are tastes that one acquires.

DALLAS: Don't you think that's a rather sentimentalized view of childhood?

WATERS: M'm. Well, yes it is, but nevertheless it's true. Children don't . . . well, actually children *do* like Molotov cocktails, of course, they do. They love Molotov cocktails. I don't know why I said that. It's clearly nonsense. They like guns and fireworks and bangs and . . . but they don't like killing. Well most of the children I know don't, anyway. Certainly my children don't. They really, really, they don't even like it in nature. They don't like it when Jon-Jon our cat kills a bird, they don't like it. Because they identify with the bird. Killing is very worrying I think to children, and it's something that we get hardened to as we grow older. Some of us get more hardened to it than others.

DALLAS: Can I ask this about your children: Do you think you've succeeded in protecting them, or not doing to them the sort of things that you depict in 'The Wall'?

WATERS: Er. So far, yeah. It depends what you're talking about. I haven't gone away and been killed in a war. Equally, you known, we've been as careful as we can to make sure that when they leave us and go away to their schools, because they both go to school now, that they're not maltreated. And also we try as much as possible to explain things to them.

The things that are done to the children in the film, well to the main character, is that his father is killed and that clearly is being done to a hell of a lot of children all over the world, apparently more and more. I mean the pace at which carnage in the world is apparently growing. There was a little bit of a lull after the end of the Vietnam conflagration but it seems to be just rising and rising and rising now. I don't know, maybe I'm becoming more sensitive to it, maybe it's not, maybe it's something that goes along on a level, but it seems to be so, clearly there are an enormous number of war orphans being created now.

DALLAS: How did you feel, when the kids in Soweto were singing 'We don't need no education'? I wondered what your reaction to that was?

WATERS: I was very pleased. I think when people are protesting about something, it's good if they've got a nice, kind of catchy tune that they can all remember, to use. To use as a sort of weapon.

I've just given permission to some people who are doing

142

a CND thing to use the tune, to write their own words to it. The Germans used it, as well, the German anti-nuclear lobby wrote their own words to it, and used the tune on marches and things. I was really pleased. I like that.

DALLAS: Can we talk about some of your earlier work, before 'The Wall', because it's a big frustration to me that we never had a chance to talk about 'Animals', which I found a very, very interesting work, and I thought the characterization of it in that Rolling Stone article particularly crass, saying that you wrote people off as pigs and sheep and dogs, but it seemed to me that was a very humanitarian statement, and I found it a very moving album.

WATERS: Good.

DALLAS: The thing that interests me, it seems to me that 'Dark Side of the Moon' and 'Wish You Were Here' are like a double album that came out in two sections. They seem to be very related to each other in theme. You may not accept this division, it may be purely artificial, but I found myself listening to 'Animals' and trying to decide whether it was the last part of that trilogy or the beginning of 'The Wall' because there's elements of both in it. Are you able to distance yourself from your past work, to look at it and say . . .

WATERS: I think 'Animals' is more to do with 'The Wall' than it was to do with 'Wish You Were Here'. In fact when I started jotting ideas down, strange ideas for a film, at one time, I did a lot of drawings using animal masks and things.

DALLAS: This was after 'The Wall' album but when you were working on the movie?

WATERS: No. No, no, no. I was working on ideas for the movie even before I started writing music for 'The Wall'. You see I actually bought a book and learnt how to write screenplays so that people could actually understand it who are in film. Clearly, this was after conversations with Scarfe and with Parker.

DALLAS: How many pages is it?

WATERS: 39 pages.

DALLAS: You were too young to do any kind of national service, weren't you?

WATERS: I was in the cadet force at school, Combined Cadet Force. I spent weekends at *HMS Ganges*.

DALLAS: You were a naval cadet?

WATERS: Yeah. I was absolutely horrified by it. I couldn't believe it.

143

I don't know if you know about *HMS Ganges*, it's for train-
ing boy sailors, kids when they're 14. Phew!

I also spent weekends on *Vanguard* before she was
scrapped, and that was pretty weird. I don't like the sea,
though, at all. I get seasick.

DALLAS: So why did you become a naval cadet?

WATERS: I couldn't bear the itching of the army uniform. I couldn't
bear it. And so I got into all that and became a Leading Sea-
man and things.

DALLAS: You did quite well, then?

WATERS: Well, yeah, I dunno why, quite. I dunno why. I liked guns,
I liked firing guns and all that stuff, in fact I used to shoot
for the school, small-bore shooting, and then I think there's
something in me that makes me want to kind of dominate
people anyway, so I did all that in the cadet force and was I
think roundly hated by most of the people involved.

In fact, one weekend I was set upon by a bunch of
enraged schoolboys and dealt with.

DALLAS: Who were under you?

WATERS: Yeah, and I learnt a lesson then, a bit. It's not a terribly
good thing to throw your weight around too much. And
then I left.

DALLAS: But don't you have a position of great authority in the
Floyd orbit?

WATERS: Yeah, and I still abuse it sometimes.

DALLAS: Do you still get set upon?

WATERS: No. Well (a) I tread more warily than I did when I was 14,
and (b) I think I probably protect myself more efficiently
than I did then. I stayed on for a third year in the sixth form,
because I'd failed one of my A levels, Applied Maths or
something, Pure Maths. Anyway, I failed something so I
stayed on for a third year, and I was the only boy in the
school in living memory who'd stayed on for a third year
in the sixth without being made a prefect, for which I'm
quite proud. My final school report said, this was all it said,
it said: 'Waters never fulfilled his considerable potential
and was dishonourably discharged from the cadet force.'

DALLAS: Is that so?

WATERS: Oh yeah, I was dishonourably discharged.

DALLAS: What, after this fracus?

WATERS: No, no, no, nothing to do with that. I just suddenly
decided I didn't want it, and you couldn't leave, it wasn't
in the rules, you weren't allowed to leave. I just handed

144

my uniform back in and said I wasn't going any more. So I was dishonourably discharged, turned out in disgrace.

Although I have said I didn't *enjoy* it, my estimation of 'The Wall' has risen in recollection, having seen the live show several times, been at the film press show and, subsequently, viewed the video version literally hundreds of times over and over.

The interesting thing is how much better the film works at home. Obviously, there is some loss in definition in the transition from 70mm celluloid to the quite differently-proportioned cathode ray tube, and even if one plays a stereo version through the home audio system, the sound doesn't have quite the same impact that full Dolby magnetic stereo can have in a big cinema.

This works in the film's favour, however, toning down some of its excessive impact that sends the cinema audience reeling out into the open air after 95 minutes of what I have called 'psychic attack'.

The disjunction of time and place, symbolised perhaps by the ubiquitous telly which, in the film, survives at least two terminal attacks, turning up on battlefields, train stations, country scenes, and almost always rerunning 'The Dambusters' (a film commemorating one of the war's worst atrocities, in which thousands of civilians were drowned to little effect on the Nazi war effort, eclipsed in its horror only by Belsen, Buchenwald, Babi Yar, Hamburg, Dresden, Hiroshima, Nagasaki). The sentimentality of the airmen lamenting the loss of Niggar, the dog, while contemplating such a horror with the impersonal efficiency of the back-room boffin, reminds us that Himmler, head of the SS, was also a sentimental man.

Such peripheral detail is used to very telling effect: the fact that the TV is showing a love scene with Stewart Granger when it is smashed is also a comment on the realities of Pink's bad relationships in the real world, the groupie who cannot get through to him, and his wife. But is this real life? There is a suggestion in what follows that the groupie is also part of his fantasy.

If it had not been made by a best-selling group and a charismatically voguish director, if it had been a grainy black-and-white New York loft production, with music by Philip Glass or Laurie Anderson, the avant garde would have taken it to its amply upholstered bosom, and the critics would have drooled as it emptied the art cinemas. Instead, it became a box-office smash – and a year later, when people were handing out their best and worst of the year awards, it didn't even get a mention. In the end, though, one is sent back to the album, which alone illustrates Roger Waters' vision undiluted and unmediated by anyone else's.

At the time it was first released, it seemed like rather expensive therapy for its composer. But as time goes by, and on repeated re-hearing (which it repays), it's clear that there are at least demons which have not yet been exorcised from Waters' psyche, if only because it is only tangentially about the hell of being a rock star, or even the hell of being any individual whose father he has never seen.

What it is about is the search for solutions, and how the attempt to solve the problem in terms presented by the problem only makes the problem greater.

The world is full of people who do this: big capitalists, gamblers, small-time crooks, lonely, tired whores, compromising trade union leaders, time-serving politicians – and, demonstrably but not any more significantly, rock stars.

The 'mad bugger' against whose wall the singer bangs his heart at the end is you and me.

THE FINAL CUT

A requiem for the post-war dream by Roger Waters
Prod by Roger Waters, James Guthrie, Michael Kamen, rec at Mayfair, Olympic, Eel Pie, Audio International, RAK, Hookend and the Billiard Room, July–Dec 1982, eng James Guthrie, Andy Jackson, ass Andy Canelle, Mike Nocito, Jules Bowen, rel March 23 1983
Michael Kamen (pno, hmnm), Andy Bown (Hammond org), Ray Cooper (perc), Andy Newmark (drs on 'Two Suns'), Raphael Ravenscroft (tnr sax), National Philharmonic Orch cond Michael Kamen

> The Post War Dream
> Your Possible Pasts
> One of the Few
> The Hero's Return
> The Gunner's Dream
> Paranoid Eyes
>
> Get Your Filthy Hands Off My Desert
> The Fletcher Memorial Home
> Southampton Dock
> The Final Cut
> Not Now John
> Two Suns in the Sunset

> *This was the most unkindest cut of all.*
> – William Shakespeare: 'Julius Caesar'

Although 'The Final Cut' must probably be accounted a failure, it is a magnificent failure. And it is interesting that it is almost the only product of the supposedly radical rock culture to have addressed itself to the traumatising events of the 1982 Falklands adventure, that was so nearly a disaster, with its recurring theme of 'Oh Maggie, what have we done?'

(The only other example I can think of is the 'Shipbuilder' single that Elvis Costello made with Robert Wyatt.)

And though the disagreements between Waters and Gilmour over it resulted in Dave's name being removed from the production credits, to the extent that he now thinks it should have been a solo album, there is a lot of Gilmour in it, including some very fine guitar, especially on the title song.

And it was Nick Mason who persuaded Roger to make the continued reprise of the 'Maggie' words instrumental, rather than a reiteration of the actual lyrics, which strengthened its contemporary relevance in a way that the more specific reference could never have done.

When it came out, Dave Gilmour told me: 'It's not how I would like to see the Pink Floyd continue. It's not what I would like to do. I didn't enjoy making it, I didn't have much to do with making it, and there was very little enjoyment in it, for me. It's made me consider saying "Oh fuck it, I'll jack it in". Because it's not what I want to do, any more. But I haven't done that, as yet. Who knows? It's one of those hard things.

'One of the things we had an enormous argument about was the fact that I was on the production credits at the beginning, and there is a certain amount of production work on it done by me. But nearly everything that I wanted to do, Roger didn't want to happen. He didn't like any of the ideas that I had. After a while I just gave up. We had an enormous fight about it and eventually I said, "Well, alright, I won't have my name on it." In the end I'm quite glad not to have my name on it.

'For Roger, as I say, it's a successful album. He's setting out to explore something, and he does it very successfully. I think, personally, it's a weak album musically. I think there's only three good songs on it. I can't quite manage to make myself believe that if the lyrics and the power of what you're saying is good enough then the music that helps portray it doesn't really matter.

'In a way it would have been better to have been a solo album, I think. It is a solo album, really, largely.'

And, when we spoke again just before his second solo album, Dave still felt much the same way: 'No, I haven't changed my views on it. I don't think it's a good album. I think there are three great tracks on it: "Fletcher", "The Gunner's Dream" and "The Final Cut", which I think are all very good tracks. I think a lot of the rest of it, and the general, over-all feel to the album is not to my taste, really. I think it's probably the weakest over-all album that we've done for quite a while. That's just an opinion.

'I'm sure Roger would disagree. I think Roger's very proud of it.' Roger was. But he, too, had his reservations later, chiefly about the quality of the singing.

'I listened to it again, very recently,' he said, 'and I really like some of it. I love all that Southampton Dock stuff, that little section, I'm really proud of that.

'But on some of it, I can hear in my voice all the strain and aggravation that was going on at the time, it affected the record.'

I objected that it was the 'strain and aggravation' during the making of 'Wish You Were Here' that contributed to the album's power.

'This strain and aggravation meant that my mind wasn't on it, not fully on it,' was his brief comment on that suggestion.

As most people probably know, it was originally planned as a soundtrack album for 'The Wall', but since most of the movie used the album tracks, plus a bit of re-recording and just one new song, there didn't seem much point in that. (Commercial point, of course: a soundtrack album would probably have shifted more units than were sold of 'The Final Cut', but they'd have received a lot of critical stick. Not that I'm suggesting they care what the critics say!)

About two thirds of the album takes the war scenes in various Pink Floyd work, culminating in 'The Wall', and attempts to make a kind of summation, and, perhaps, an acknowledgement of guilt for the betrayal of what the album calls 'the postwar dream', the betrayal of soldiers like his father. He said of the album to me: 'It says something about a sense, I suppose for me personally, a sense that *I* may have betrayed him. He died in the last war and I kind of feel that I personally may have betrayed him, because we haven't managed to improve things very much. That the economic cycles still over-ride everything, with the best intentions, the cycle of economic recession followed by resurgence still governs our actions.

'So everything's accelerating, and it seems very likely that we'll just get into one big down and that'll be the end of it. We'll get into a great big down and somebody somewhere, by some mistake or just because they think it seems like a good idea, will press the button and that'll be the end.

'I see no way round that, unless we stop having quite so many children. Do you?'

I've dealt elsewhere with the lyrical content of most of the songs, but I'd like to take issue with Gilmour about the album's musical strength,

148

which grows more powerful to me every time I hear it. The songs seem to have an organic relationship to each other which fully justifies seeing the album as a complete work, rather than just a collection of melodies which happen to be neighbours upon it. And if ever an album needed the compact digital disc to get past the cottonwool and fluff that seems to clog up even the best systems for reproducing vinyl records, it is this one. The sound effects, for instance, use a system devised by Hugo Zuccarelli called 'holophonics', based on a radically different (and controversial) approach to a theory of sound, which makes them come blasting off the disc; but on the conventional analogue disc much of their impact is lost.

The two songs which seem outside the 'postwar requiem' theme are 'Not Now John', which was issued as a single in a somewhat bowdlerised form, and 'Two Suns in the Sunset', about the Bomb.

I agree with Gilmour when he says he doesn't think the first is a very good song. 'I don't like that at all,' he says, bluntly, and suggests that it was only issued in response to record company pressure.

However, it *is* an important song in relation to the complex nature of its composer, and is saying something he himself believes when he dismisses all the album till then with the curt expletive: 'Fuck all that!' In 1982, we saw how Roger was talking about the schizophrenic character of 'Wish You Were Here' and the divisions in his own nature which it reflected: 'There's the bit that's concerned with other people, the bit that one applauds in oneself, then there's the grasping avaricious, selfish little kid who wants to get his hands on the sweets and have them all.'

That is the singer of this particular song.

The final song brings the reality of what's been done since the war right to centre stage, because it's not merely about loyalty to past generations; it's also about loyalty to the future.

In the song, the writer is travelling home into the sunset, and he sees another sun rising in his driving mirror. The words are his thoughts of regret as he dies.

During the war, at the height of the last ditch flying bomb offensive by Hitler's cruise missiles against Southern England, I was flat on my back in a hospital bed in Carshalton Beeches. As I lay out there in the sun, I heard that strangulated diesel sound of the V1 rocket coming towards me and I saw it getting larger and larger. The engine cut out, and I saw the nose drop and point straight at me.

I closed my eyes and composed myself for death. I was not afraid; the strongest emotion I felt was regret at the waste of a life that was only 14 years long, at that time. Nearly 40 years later, I can still feel the bitterness of that feeling, though the bomb actually landed 100 yards away from my bed and all I felt was the breeze of the bomb blast.

So I feel I can empathise with what the character in the song feels, the resigned anger at the terrible waste of it all.

Roger told me how he came to write it. 'That was a thought I had, driving home one night, thinking: We all sit around and talk about the possibility of "accidents" or as I put it in the song people just getting so bloody angry that finally somebody pushes a button. Well the song's all about that moment when suddenly it happens, you know it's happened and you know it's the end, you're dead, and it's the end of the world, and that you'll never see your kids again or your wife or anybody that you love and it's all over.

'It's very easy to go: "Oh yes, well there may be an accident and the holocaust may happen", without having the feeling of what it might be like.

'And that's why it says in the song *and as the windscreen melts my tears evaporate leaving only charcoal to defend, finally I understand the feelings of The Few* (Winston Churchill's name for the RAF), which is supposed to be a reference to the bomber and the gunner and all those people, my dad, and all the other war casualties.

'That song, I suppose, in a way is going back to the second song on the album where there's a line, *a warning to anyone still in command of their possible futures: Take care.*'

If this was really the Floyd's last album, it wouldn't have been a bad epitaph to have bequeathed to the world.

150

PART FOUR

Outside The Wall

BRICK VIII
The Solo Albums

Ain't life a solo?
–Sandy Denny

SYD BARRETT: The Madcap Laughs
Prod David Gilmour & Roger Waters (6 tracks prod Malcolm Jones).
Rec EMI Studios, Abbey Road, London, Rel January 1970

Terrapin (prod Malcolm Jones)
No Good Trying (prod Malcolm Jones)
Love You (prod Malcolm Jones)
No Man's Land (prod Malcolm Jones)
Dark Globe (prod David Gilmour, Roger Waters)
Here I Go (prod Malcolm Jones)

Octopus (prod David Gilmour, Roger Waters)
Golden Hair (words: James Joyce) prod David Gilmour,
   Roger Waters)
Long Gone (prod David Gilmour, Roger Waters)
She Took a Long Cold Look (prod David Gilmour, Roger
   Waters)
Feel (prod David Gilmour, Roger Waters)
It It's In You (prod David Gilmour, Roger Waters)
Late Night (prod Malcolm Jones)

Octopus/Golden Hair rel as single December 1969

SYD BARRETT: Barrett
Prod David Gilmour & Richard Wright. Rec EMI Studios, Abbey
Road, London. Rel November 1970
Barrett (vocs, gtr) w Dave Gilmour (bs, 12–str gtr, org, drs), Rick
Wright (org, pno, harmonium), Jerry Shirley (drs, perc), Willy Wilson
(drs), Vic Saywell (tuba)

Baby Lemonade
Love Song
Dominoes
It Is Obvious
Rats
Maisie

Gigolo Aunt
Waving My Arms in the Air/I Never Lied to You
Wined and Dined
Wolfpack
Effervescing Elephant
All comp Syd Barrett

ROGER WATERS (with Ron Geesin): Music from 'The Body'
Prod Roger Waters & Ron Geesin. Rel December 1970

Our Song (Waters, Geesin)
Sea Shell and Stone (Waters)
Red Stuff Writhe (Geesin)
A Gentle Breeze Blew Through Life (Geesin)
Lick Your Partners (Geesin)
Bridge Passage for Three Plastic Teeth (Geesin)
Chain of Life (Waters)
The Womb Bit (Waters, Geesin)
Embryo Thought (Geesin)
March Past of the Embryos (Geesin)
More Than Seven Dwarfs in Penis-Land (Geesin)
Dance of the Red Corpuscles (Geesin)

Body Transport (Water, Geesin)
Hand Dance – Full Evening Dress (Geesin)
Beathe (Waters)
Old Folks Ascension (Geesin)
Bed-Time-Dream-Clime (Geesin)
Piddle in Perspex (Geesin)
Embryonic Womb-Walk (Geesin)
Mrs Throat Goes Walking (Geesin)
Sea Shell and Soft Stone (Waters, Geesin)
Give Birth to a Smile (Waters)

DAVID GILMOUR: David Gilmour
Prod David Gilmour at Super Bear, France. Rel May 25, 1978
Gilmour (voc, gtrs), w Rick Wells (bs), Willie Wilson (drs)

> Mihalis (Gilmour)
> There's No Way Out of Here (Baker)
> Cry from the Street (Gilmour, Stuart)
> So Far Away (Gilmour)
>
> Short and Sweet (Gilmour, Harper)
> Raise My Rent (Gilmour)
> No Way (Gilmour)
> Deafinitely (Gilmour)
> I Can't Breathe Any More (Gilmour)

RICHARD WRIGHT: Wet Dream
Prod by Richard Wright at Super Bear, France, January 1978. Rel May 1978
Wright (vocs, kbds) w Mel Collins (sax, flute), Snowy White (gtrs), Larry Steele (bs), Reg Isadore (drs)

> Mediterranean C (R. Wright)
> Against the Odds (R. Wright, J. Wright)
> Cat Cruise (R. Wright)
> Summer Elegy (R. Wright)
> Waves (R. Wright)
>
> Holiday (R. Wright)
> Mad Yannis Dance (R. Wright)
> Drop in From the Top (R. Wright)
> Pink's Song (J. Wright)
> Funky Deux (R. Wright)

NICK MASON: Nick Mason's Fictitious Sports
Prod by Nick Mason & Carla Bley. Rec at Grog Kill Studio, Willow, NY by Michael Mantler, ass Nick Mason, in Oct 1979, mixed by James Guthrie in Dec 1979 and May 1980. Rel 1980
Mason (drs, perc) w Robert Wyatt (vocs), Karen Kraft (vocs), Chris Spedding (gtrs), Carla Bley (kbds), Gary Windo (tnr sax, bs clart, flute), Gary Valente (tmbs), Mike Mantler (tpts), Howard Johnson (tuba), Steve Swallow (bs), Terry Adams (pno, harmonica, Clavinet),

Gary Windo, Carlos Ward, D. Sharpe, Gary Valente, Vincent Chancey, Earl MacIntyre (additional vocs)
All words and music by Carla Bley

> Can't Get My Motor to Start
> I Was Wrong
> Siam
> Hot River

> Boo to You Too
> Do Ya?
> Wervin'
> I'm a Mineralist

DAVID GILMOUR: About Face
Prod by Bob Ezrin & David Gilmour. Rec by Andrew Jackson & Kit Woolven at Pathe-Marconi, Paris. Rel March 5, 1984
Gilmour (gtr, vocs), w Jeff Porcaro (drs, perc), Pino Palladino (bs gtr), Ian Kewley (Hammon org, pno) and Steve Winwood (pno, org), Anne Dudley (synth), Bob Ezrin (kbds), Louis Jardine (perc), Ray Cooper (perc), Jon Lord (synth), the Kick Horns (Roddy Lorimer, Barbara Snow, Tim Sanders, Simon Clerk), National Philharmonic Orch arr by Michael Kamen w Bob Ezrin, Vicki & Sam Brown, Mickey Feat and Roy Harper (backing vocs), Steve Rance (Fairlight programming)

> Until We Sleep (David Gilmour)
> Murder (David Gilmour)
> Love on the Air (P. Townsend, David Gilmour)
> Blue Light (David Gilmour)
> Out of the Blue (David Gilmour)

> All Lovers Are Deranged (P. Townsend, David Gilmour)
> You Know I'm Right (David Gilmour)
> Cruise (David Gilmour)
> Let's Get Metaphysical (David Gilmour)
> Near the End (David Gilmour)

ZEE: Identity
Prod Richard Wright, Dave Harris, co-prod & eng Tim Palmer. Rel April 9 1984
Wright (kbds, backing vocs, perc, Fairlight), Harris (gtrs, lead vocs, kbds, perc, Fairlight)

Confusion (Wright, Harris)
Voices (Wright, Harris)
Private Person (Wright, Harris)
Strange Rhythm (Wright, Harris)
Eyes of a Gypsy (Harris)

Cuts Like a Diamond (Wright, Harris)
By Touching (Wright, Harris)
How Do You Do It (Wright, Harris)
Seems We Were Dreaming (Wright, Harris)

ROGER WATERS: The Pros and Cons of Hitch Hiking
Written Roger Waters. Prod Roger Waters & Michael Kamen. Eng
Andy Jackson. Rec Olymipic, Eel Pie & the Billiard Room Feb–Dec
1983. Rel April 30 1984
Waters (vocs, rh gtr, bs), w Andy Brown (Hammon org, synth), Ray
Cooper (perc), Eric Clapton (lead gtr), Michael Kamen (pno), Andy
Newmark (drs), David Sanborn (sax), Madeleine Bell, Katie Kissoon,
Doreen Chandler (backing vocs), Raphael Ravenscroft, Kevin
Flanagan, Vic Sullivan (horns)

4.30pm	(Apparently They Were Travelling Abroad)
4.37am	(Arabs With Knives and West German Skies)
4.39am	(For the First Time Today, Part 2)
4.41am	(Sexual Revolution)
4.47am	(The Remains of Our Love)
4.50am	(Go Fishing)
4.56am	(For the First Time Today, Part 1)
4.58am	(Dunroamin, Duncarin, Dunlivin)
5.01am	(The Pros and Cons of Hitch Hiking, Part 10)
5.06am	(Every Stranger's Eyes)
5.11am	(The Moment of Clarity)

None of the solo work of the members of Pink Floyd amounted to
much until the very future of the band came into doubt. Syd Barrett's
'Madcap' may be an underground classic dating back to the early
Seventies – but he'd left the band already then.

And the Gilmour and Wright albums of '78 are probably more
symptomatic of the post-'Animals' malaise that infected most of the
band than any genuine solo ambitions. Rick, by that time, had
continued to lose interest in what was happening, and indeed it was his
lack of enthusiasm for the 'Wall' project – most of the best keyboard

work on the album comes from session players – that caused him to be ejected from the group.

Though he was fairly defensive about it at the time, Gilmour had obviously sought in his first to find a more spontaneous approach to music.

'I don't think the Floyd's music is too well-conceived,' he told me, then. 'I like to work that way, but if to put that amount of work and thought into it means that you lose spontaneity or immediacy then that's a shame. But, at the same time, it's nice to have more than one direction to what you're doing. It's nice for me to have an alternative which is different, at least in the attitude and the way I'm going about it, even if some of it comes out sounding a little bit similar.

'The scope for musical freedom is getting less. There's always places where you can have a 'blow', sort of thing, but it's always the same places, all the time, and consequently they start getting a bit predictable.

'My attitude is that we sometimes get a little too stuck in the presentation of the idea and the balance is slightly tipped too far in that direction for my liking. Not *much* too much, but I'd prefer to see a little more freer area for playing.'

On balance, Gilmour's first album wasn't that remarkable, with the exception of 'Short and Sweet', a song he wrote with Roy Harper, with typically Harperish lyrics:

> *and we*
> *we the immoral men*
> *we dare*
> *naked and fearless in the elements*
> *we're free . . .*

Actually, Harper's own recording of the song on 'The Unknown Soldier' album, with Gilmour soloing, is far stronger, which is hardly surprising, because it must be even more difficult for someone else to sing Roy Harper than to sing Roger Waters.

Nick Mason's 1981 solo is a bit of an oddity. Actually, I like it very much but it's really a Carla Bley album with Nick playing drums and percussion. It illustrates the way he will adopt protective coloration, regardless of the musical context, and also the way his own musical tastes veer towards the more experiemental.

Carlos Ward, who crops up in the backing vocalists, is presumably the associate of Abdullah Ibrahim (Dollar Brand), the great South African jazz pianist.

The character of the album is very similar to that of the three Robert

158

Wyatt albums Nick produced in the mid-to-late Seventies, notably the superb 'Rock Bottom'.

At the time of 'The Final Cut', everyone was denying any split, though Roger admitted that communication between them was 'not very good'. But he was particularly irritated by an article that appeared in a London daily paper, rehashing an interview he'd done very much against his will in Rolling Stone, in which the writer drew the conclusion that the band was on its last legs.

'*All I said was* that there wasn't any reason why at some point in the future I shouldn't work with another drummer or another guitarist, or anybody,' he exclaimed. 'Of course there isn't. Dave and Nick have both made solo albums and they've worked with other drummers or other bass players or other writers, but they make it sound as if I'm saying that's the end of the band, which is nonsense.'

After 'The Final Cut', however, both Dave and Roger released solo albums, and there seemed little likelihood of further work together.

It was a time for searching the lyrics for clues. Dave's second album, a really powerful production with two songs co-written with the Who's Peter Townsend, had at least two lyrics that could be applicable to the situation in the band, 'Near the End' and 'You Know I'm Right'. Of course they could be just songs about a romance that's ending.

> *Standing in silence, holding my breath*
> *disconnected and dry*
> *and though I'm certain that there's nothing left*
> *to hold on to, to give or to try*
> *Some things never change, no don't ever change*
> *and I'm feeling the cold*
> *thinking that we're getting older and wiser*
> *when we're just getting old.*
>
> *and when you feel you're near the end*
> *and what once burned so bright is growing dim*
> *and when you see what's been achieved*
> *is there a feeling that you've been deceived?*
>
>   – 'Near the End'
>
> *Now we survey this silent battleground*
> *recriminations all around*
> *and still no compromise is found*
>
> *Now we really seem to have a problem*
> *and it won't just disappear*
> *and all the friends we thought we could rely on*
> *just want to whisper in my ear*

It's just a matter of opinions
you know you keep both in sight
why should you bother with the other side
When you know yours is right?

            –'You Know I'm Right'

Dave told me that neither was originally addressed to Roger, and 'Near the End' wasn't at all, but 'You Know I'm Right' had ended up that way despite his own intentions.

'It started off being about any situation with any person,' he said. 'I mean, it's not about Roger, it's really not, no parts of it are specifically about Roger. Some of it could apply to Roger but it didn't start off from that point of view and I really wouldn't want to do a thing whining about our relationship and the arguments and things that we've had.

'It started off being about a girl, a relationship. I'd done the first verse and that's all I had, and someone looked at it and said "That's about Roger, isn't it?" and it absolutely wasn't, at that point. But that had blown it, because I'd still got to write the rest of the song, and from that moment on, it was impossible to get on with writing the rest of the song without that coming back into mind, so there are some little jokes in there, but that's all it is, just little jokes that could apply to him, in-jokes, you wouldn't know them, things we've argued about. It's pointless to discuss that sort of thing.

'"Near the End" is about being near the end of anything you like, really, about life I suppose is what it is. Each one of the verses has a sort of double thing to it. The first verse is like talking to the person who's listening to the record, *will you just turn it over and start again?* means 'will you just turn the record over and play it again?' so there's a sort of double meaning on that one.

'The second one is about a girl friend, about the end of a relationship, and the third one is about the end of your own life, really, *what once burned so bright is growing dim* is your own life spark, I suppose.' Interestingly, although Dave shares a lot of Roger's political views he's always been rather unhappy about expressing them through his music. He has two songs about the arms race, 'Cruise', a satirical song about Ronald Reagan's wonder weapon that pretends to agree *we both know you're the best, saving our children, saving our land* and 'Out of the Blue', a rather pessimistic song about the end of the world.

Zee is a recording project put together by Rick Wright and Dave Harris of the Birmingham modernist band, Fashion, after Rick left the Floyd. It's a pleasant-enough sounding album, in the insubstantial, sequencer-dominated style of its time, but hardly memorable. 'Cuts Like a Diamond' sounds a bit like the Floyd; in fact, Harris's guitar on

160

this track could almost be Dave Gilmour.

You'll search in vain through Roger's 'The Pros and Cons of Hitch Hiking' for any clues about the future of the band, because this is far from its concerns.

Here's what I wrote at the time of its release:

> The first thing that's immediately apparent is that, however much talk there's been, including some mutinous rumblings within the band itself, about Floyd's albums becoming expressions of Waters' own ego since 'Wish You Were Here', when Waters actually comes out and makes a personal statement like this, he does it in a way that is as distinct from the sound of Floyd as he himself is from a heavy extrovert axeman like Gilmour.
>
> And the next is that, once the fickle public (and the even more fickle critics) have got used to the idea that Waters solo is a completely different animal from Waters as the Floyd lyricist and conceptualist, he emerges as a radically original performer who has something to say about the world today, and in a way that has very little to do with the fads that dominate the charts.
>
> Whether this makes him ahead of his time or a decade behind it is perhaps for you to say, because this is an album that's intended to 'say something', and if that causes you to yawn gently behind your hand and turn away, then so be it, because there's no getting away from the fact by concentrating on such peripheral matters as the playing of guest star Eric Clapton (brilliant though that is).
>
> While the Sixties concept album was responsible for a lot of pretentious dross, to be sure, the fact is that it did liberate the rock musician from the moon-and-June imbecilities of Tin Pan Alley pop, to which today's pretty boys of both sexes seem determined to return us. And whatever the failings of 'The Final Cut' – which it's my firm belief will be reassessed within the decade as a far better work than the poor sales would seem to indicate – it is remarkable that it was the *only* album that attempted to deal courageously with the trends that will turn Britain into Western Europe's first genuine police state if someone doesn't wake up pretty damn soon.
>
> In a way, 'The Pros and Cons of Hitch Hiking' is about escape from the realities of 'The Wall' and 'The Final Cut', for it's about dreams – most of which turn into nightmares.
>
> The male sexual fantasy of picking up the nubilely available girl on the road, the macho horror of suddenly being

surrounded during the act of sex itself by avenging Third World hordes, complete with castrating scimitars, the hippie 'good life' fantasy of getting it together in the country, which inevitably turns into a season of rotting crops, bunged-up septic tanks, the bizarre dream of being urged by Yoko Ono to find fulfilment by leaping from the wing of a plane, and . . . over and over . . . the fear of being alone. Dream takes place within dream, like a set of Chinese boxes or Russian dolls or the layers of the onion, until the final isolation becomes unavoidable.

We've been here before, of course, and despite the break with the past which the album's musical style and approach to its material represents, Waters is constantly hinting at past triumphs as if to establish musical links within his listeners' minds, whether it be the barely-heard murmurings of the paranoid voices on 'Dark Side of the Moon', or the descending cadence of the power chords at the beginning of 'The Wall's' 'In the Flesh'.

Each of the eleven tracks is fixed in real time by its title, from the opening '4.30am' to the closing '5.11am', so that it actually occupies less objective time than it takes to play the album – like those waking dreams which seem to encompass a whole lifetime between the first jangle of the alarm and the cold feel of the foot on the bedside lino.

Like all such dreams, it has its own mad coherence: picking up the girl from the roadside and eying her legs as the wind blows up her skirt, waking from the nightmare (though still in the dream), and deciding to get away from it all into the paradise of Wyoming, the inevitable unfaithfulness with the visitor from the city, and then finally the waking, with the reassurance of the real feminine presence at your side, not the tempting chimera of the dream but the real companion for life, with the reassuring final words: *I couldn't take another moment alone.*

As such, it will no doubt translate into vivid concrete images for the touring stage show, but it's really a journey in the mind, which the tortured, despairing vocals and often exultant, serene music counterpointing it, makes into something as powerful and, in many ways, as hard to take as a Charles Munch painting of a screaming mouth.

It could be depressing, if it wasn't for that musical counterpoint: some of the most beautiful playing to come from Clapton since the days of 'Layla', and equally magnificent sax from New York's funk idol, David Sanborne.

And it needs to be realised that, while for many of today's pop stars dreams are the means of escape from reality, in Waters' vision it is the dream which he finally succeeds in escaping from, and reality which is the refuge.

The only jarring note in the whole affair is represented by the the title song, with its jaunty, bluesy melody and chirpy back-up singers (led by the lovely-voiced Madeleine Bell), which is so up it seems like a barefaced attempt to hit the charts in the way that the Floyd's last single, 'Not Now John', singularly failed to do.

Musically, it works well enough, but it is so out of character with the rest of the album that it falls through the middle, and only just avoids throwing the entire balance out. As a single (for such it is), it could make the American AOR FM stations, and there's a lovely moment in the middle where a reference to Shane is echoed by the young boy's voice from the end of the Alan Ladd movie, but the whole track's like an interlude shoved in to appease the record industry bosses, which would be a strange ploy, coming from such a determinedly successful maverick as Waters.

The judgement of the future on this album may not be very kind, I suspect. But it will have to be respected as the work which marked out Roger Waters' determination to be his own man, having put the collective angst of Floyd behind him.

His second solo album, I predict, will blow your wig off.

The album was followed by a tour, which would seem to indicate that Waters intends the future of Floyd to be in his solo career. Though not as complex as 'The Wall' technically, it was presented in the same sort of halls, and used Gerald Scarfe's back projections to great effect.

The least successful part of the proceedings, surprisingly, was the first half, which consisted of a run-through of Floyd's greatest hits. Even the back-projections had a somewhat worn and tatty air, as if they'd outlived their usefulness and weren't being too well protected – or projected. The first of the two Earls Court concerts was less than overwhelming, and Roger was so dischuffed about it that he refused to do an encore, and was positively grumpy back-stage afterwards. The second was tighter and more impressive, and after the enormously impressive live performance of 'Hitch Hiking', he ended with 'Brain Damage'.

On this showing, neither of the ex-colleagues is doing as well on his own as he did as part of the team, with Roger getting closer to remaking a solo career than any of the others.

Horses for Courses, Market Forces

The story since then

They're the powers that be
They like a bomb-proof Cadillac
Air-conditioned, gold taps,
Back-seat gun rack, platinum hub caps
They pick horses for courses
They are the market forces . . .

– Roger Waters, The Powers That Be
(from Radio K.A.O.S.)

He has laughed and he has cried
He has fought and he has died
He's just the same as all the rest
He's not the worst, he's not the best

He's haunted by the memory of a lost paradise
In his youth or in a dream, he can't be precise
He's chained forever to a world that's departed
It's not enough, it's not enough

– Dave Gilmour
(from Yet Another Movie and Sorrow,
two songs on the new Floyd album)

Shit! but suddenly the phone starts ringing.

Roger Waters, first, out of the blue, so I didn't even have the recorder running, but as I remember it, the talk goes something like this:

ROGER: Remember you said Pro's and Cons seemed like a transitional album? Well, I've finished the new one and I think you may have been right, 'cos it's rather fucking great.

KARL: So when can we talk?

ROGER: I'd like you to hear it first, so I'm biking a tape over.

KARL: Great (etc etc).

Then I bump into Gilmour at a preview of some paintings by his wife, Ginger. He tells me Floyd are about halfway through their new album

164

and expect to tour in the autumn.

'Of course,' he says, 'Roger's trying to fuck it all up,' which was the first intimation that the agreement to disagree back in the days of 'The Final Cut' has finally blossomed into actual antagonism with, I was later to learn, the full panoply of the law being brought to bear.

Then Roger again, this time by arrangement, and the tape is running, only we never get round to doing much more than talk about talking. Halfway through a question about the stage show, he interrupts himself: 'Listen, just before we go on Karl, I have to say that I'm a bit leary about committing myself to your book, a long interview for your book, in the light of what's going on with Dave and Nick.'

KARL: Well they're in LA, as you know.

ROGER: Yes, I know.

KARL: So I haven't had a chance to talk to them.

ROGER: And I believe they'll be in LA for some time, now.

KARL: Yes, so I gather.

ROGER: But they've also, I don't know if you know or not, put concerts on sale in Canada.

KARL: Yes, that I do know.
I don't want . . . well basically I want to talk about the album and how you'll be representing that album on tour and then, if you've got anything to say on it, I'd like to hear a little about what's been going down between you and Dave, but that's by far a lower priority because basically you know my position is, I'm really fairly uninterested in these sort of inter-group . . . I'm interested in music, do you understand?

ROGER: Yes, absolutely.

KARL: Obviously, the 'business' impinges on the music, usually to its detriment, and one can't ignore it.

ROGER: All right, if I'm talking to you about the show and the record and all that kind of thing, are we talking about your book?

KARL: We're talking about whatever use I can make of it. The book and other media as well, but until we've finished talking I don't know what the marketability of it is, as it were. My prime concern is with the book because I want it to be up to date when it comes out.

ROGER: OK, before we go any further, I would like you to clear anything that you sell it to, with me.

KARL: Yes, that's fine.

ROGER: And (long pause) you may think I'm being very very, very weedy and maybe I am, but I can't tell you the aggravation,

165

and I won't tell you the aggravation, because as you say, it's none of your business, it's not very interesting to other people, really.

And so on and so on.

The upshot of it all was that we never spoke again, on that or any other subject, partly because I was so pissed off at the rise in the paranoia count since the previous time we'd conversed.

Roger has always claimed the right to check transcripts of our various chats, and make amendments as he thought fit with the benefit of hindsight, and I went along with this, though it's a right I have never granted anyone else.

But to have to clear with him where I sell the results?

Five minutes after I put down the phone, and despite my too-ready agreement, I was thinking, in the immortal words of Pamela Zarubica, also known as Suzy Creemcheeze: Forget it!

So rather than renege on a deal, I made only desultory attempts to reach him, and never actually managed it. Which didn't worry me, terribly, because having heard his album, I was a bit more concerned to see if Dave and Nick and Rick could manage better without him than he was doing without them.

Cut to four in the afternoon a couple of weeks later and it's eight in the morning in Los Angeles. Dave is on the phone and taking care of a few bits of business before he goes into the studio for his daily twelve-hour stint, bits like talking to this arsehole from London who's got this boring book to finish.

Here's how it goes. We start talking about the album, but before we finish, business and the law rear their ugly heads.

DAVE: I think there's going to be about eight titles on it, along with various sorts of bits which are untitleable.

KARL: Is it vocal or instrumental or what?

DAVE: Yeah, it's songs, you know the usual sort of record, with loud guitars and voices and all the usual things. What can one say?

KARL: So if you've got that many songs, they're all fairly short, you haven't got any long epics?

DAVE: Well, they run out up to six–seven minutes long, some of 'em.

KARL: Who's written most of them?

DAVE: Well, I've written most of it with a couple of other people helping out, Bob Ezrin who's co-producing with me has written a little bit of it, a guy called Anthony Moore has co-written three lyrics with me.

166

KARL:	That's the guy who worked with Slapp Happy for a while, isn't it?
DAVE:	I think so, yeah.
KARL:	And the music?
DAVE:	The music was mostly written by me. One, a couple of bits were co-written with a couple of other people.
KARL:	The couple of other people not being Rick and Nick.
DAVE:	No, Rick and Nick haven't got any writing credits on it.
KARL:	And have you been working in the usual Pink Floyd way, sort of exploring the way things go, without any pre-conceived idea or where you're going?
DAVE:	We spent a long time, yes, just throwing things around in the studio in England.
KARL:	Which studio was that?
DAVE:	My studio I've got in Hampstead.
KARL:	I see.
	When was that, actually?
DAVE:	We started in October, I think it was. We've been working with a computer, doing MIDI recording on a computer, which has been quite fun, a new experience.
KARL:	What computer was that?
DAVE:	An Apple Macintosh.
KARL:	What instruments have you been inputting to the MIDI live: guitar, keyboards?
DAVE:	Well, from guitar, from drums, and from keyboards. We've got a guitar synthesizer sort of thing, some Simmonds drums that speak a MIDI language so to speak. It's very easy to manipulate songs and work on that system because you can actually use your demos as masters, which is quite fun.
KARL:	So Pink Floyd get closer to living up to their space-age reputation. You've always had this technological reputation but your stuff has really been terribly traditional in the way it's laid down, hasn't it?
DAVE:	Yes this is true. A lot of things get tried with the Floyd but the actual instruments in the end are the usual old kind of things, real drums and guitars and Hammond organs and voices and things.
KARL:	I assume you're doing all the vocals.
DAVE:	Well, Rick does a couple of harmony vocals and bits and pieces but I'm doing all the lead vocals.
KARL:	What guitar are you using most of the time?
DAVE:	Mostly Fender Stratocasters.
KARL:	You told me yesterday you couldn't tell me the actual title

of the album. I assume that's still the situation.

DAVE: Yes, it is. We're still arguing about it. We have a title, but one or two of us . . . it hasn't been printed yet, and until it's printed there'll still be some dissent.

KARL: You say one or two people don't agree. There's only three of you.

DAVE: Yes, but there are lots of other opinions that one respects.

KARL: You mean, like Steve (O'Rourke, the Floyd's manager)?

DAVE: Well, there's Steve, there's Bob Ezrin who's co-producing. Anyone else who's around who feels like throwing their oar in, I'll welcome their opinions.

KARL: I'll give you mine if you'll tell me what you're arguing about.

DAVE: Well, at the moment we're calling it 'A Momentary Lapse of Reason'. But some people think it's a bit too much of a mouthful for a pop record. But that's the working title for the moment.

KARL: 'A Momentary Lapse' might be a good abbreviation. It gives the critics all sorts of opportunities to be snide, but when did they ever need that?

DAVE: Well, some of the other ones that people came up with were much worse in that area. Someone suggested calling it 'Signs of Life', but I thought Yeah, yeah, we'll really get some trouble on that one. No sign of life here.

KARL: Who thought of that title originally?

DAVE: I did.

KARL: Can you tell me the songs?

DAVE: There's a song called 'Sorrow'.

KARL: And what's the sorrow about? I mean, obviously it's about sorrow, but what kind of sorrow?

DAVE: I dunno, Karl, I could read you the lyric if you like. Work it out for yourself.
(He does so.)
Pretty poetic, eh?
We've got one called 'Yet Another Movie'.

KARL: Is that using the term in a metaphorical sense?

DAVE: Um, it's in the realms of fantasy, slightly. It's a sort of, I wouldn't know how to describe it, really. It's a hard one to describe, because it's a new kind of departure for me, I think.

KARL: What kind of departure?

DAVE: In the way of writing, for me. I'm not a particularly experienced lyric writer, over the years, and I find myself tending to limit myself to songs which are of direct personal experience to me. I'm trying to find a way of moving out into areas that are both interesting to me and kind of, I suppose poetic, but taking you out of the realms of just what you think about love and life and death and so on which tend to preoccupy me, as well as a great many other people. We're getting into areas of fiction where we're sort of observing other things or even writing things which are slightly in the area of fantasy. It's like a new area for me. It's hard to tell.

KARL: OK, what else is there?

DAVE: There's one called 'A New Machine'.

KARL: Anything like 'Welcome to the Machine'?

DAVE: Nothing like it.

KARL: No cross-reference, or anything like that?

DAVE: No, not really, it just happened to come out like that. There's one called 'Terminal Frost', which is an instrumental.

KARL: How would you describe the general mood of the album? Up, down?

DAVE: Up and down. It's not a case of prolonged misery, like 'The Final Cut', (laughs) it's certainly not lightweight, either. I don't know. If one had to describe what areas of Pink Floyd music it's closest to, it's in the 'Wish You Were Here' period, more than I'd put it in 'The Wall' period, if you like.

KARL: Are there any lyrics which are or might be construed to be a commentary on what's been happening to the Floyd since, shall we say, 'The Final Cut'?

DAVE: Um . . . no. No.

KARL: I'm thinking that there was a song on your solo album that started off being not about and then became about Roger, didn't it?

DAVE: Yeah, became partly about him. You know I'm not wasting my time thinking about what Roger's doing or his problems. He's still got to work his own problems out. I've got the rest of my life and career to get on with and I can't be bothered with him. It's all in the past, all that stuff, except that I still have to deal with some legal factors to do with it all. But as far as we're concerned, it's just history . . . Roger has been saying for some time that he'd like to knock it all on the head, but I've been saying that I'd like to do it again. There are avenues open to me under the name of

	Pink Floyd that I still enjoy that I can't do any other way, and I like it. So I see no reason to stop it, while I still enjoy it.
KARL:	How did it happen that Rick rejoined you?
DAVE:	I thought it would make us stronger legally and musically in terms of creating areas of recognisable Floyd songs. If there's an air of doubt and disbelief in the minds of the public out there, which has been generated by someone else's slanging, it's very valuable to have more strength on your side, if we can create something that sounds more like Pink Floyd, that's good. I mean, I like the stuff that Rick does, when he does it well.
KARL:	You yourself commented that he contributed very little to 'The Wall'.
DAVE:	Yes, he didn't contribute very much to 'The Wall', this is true. He hasn't contributed an awful lot to this record, but there are some specific bits where, you know, his contribution is a valuable one.
KARL:	That only he could have done.
DAVE:	Yeah.
KARL:	Did you approach him, to ask him to come back, or, how did it happen?
DAVE:	I can't remember exactly what happened. I know he heard that we were doing something and when we were in Greece last summer he was pushed by his new wife into suggesting that he'd be interested in contributing in some way.
KARL:	So what is the nature of the dispute with Roger? Presumably Pink Floyd is a co-operative, a jointly-owned thing between the four of you.
DAVE:	Pink Floyd Music is a company of which Roger and Rick are both still shareholders and directors and Pink Floyd Music has since 1972 or 73 been the force, the company force behind the processes that go on, that pays the wages, that receives the royalties, that distributes the royalties, the contracts with the record company are with. So everyone who's been in the group at any one particular time since the early Seventies has been a shareholder and director, and they own rights in all the stuff to which they have contributed.

Now Roger left, in December 1985, of his own free will, left the group Pink Floyd. He sent letters to the record companies informing them of his decision and asked to be released of the obligations he had as a member of Pink

Floyd to them, and he's allowed to continue on with his solo career projects under the terms of the contract which provided for that. He then, having done that, declared that Pink Floyd was over. I declared that it wasn't.

Basically, his dispute with us is that he has declared that Pink Floyd has ceased to exist, and we haven't the right to use the name. In my view, if someone leaves a rock 'n' roll group, as they inevitably will, then that doesn't mean that everyone else has to leave, too. The legal side of it is that he's got a writ against the company or something, trying to clarify all this stuff, which should come to court in about a year's time, I imagine.

KARL: So, he's still a director of Pink Floyd Music?

DAVE: Yeah.

KARL: And the contract with EMI is between Pink Floyd Music and EMI. So will the new album come under that aegis or is it being done through a different company?

DAVE: Well, at the moment it's being done through the same company, because we cannot as yet, until all these things get cleared up, form a new company and do it all under a new thing which would be very nice. Because at the moment we have to have a board meeting for every single decision we want to do as a group, virtually, and Roger comes and he votes against it, and me and Nick vote for it, and basically it's a pain in the arse.

The effort of moving forward, of changing the CBS contracts so that they pay myself and Nick the royalties for this record, the hundreds of different things that we have to do, all have to go through Pink Floyd board meetings, to which Roger comes and votes against everything that we want to do.

In the normal case, when everyone's in agreement, we don't have to have board meetings, we just ring each other up and say shall we do this and we say fine, and we just carry on. We enter a note that we all decided to do this and we can get on with things. This way means that every process that we want to do, by having to hold board meetings, with reasonable notice, because we have to stick with the legal requirements and Roger's just being very, very obstructionist.

You see how the business gets in the way. With the best will in the world, you can't avoid it, and the pleasing thing is that, with all that aggro, Dave and Nick and Rick (and Tom Scott and Pat Leonard and Scott Page and John Carin), have produced some rather vintage Floyd.

The other alternative title for the new Floyd album is 'Of Promises Broken' (the argument continues as I write this) and here, again, one is tempted to apply the lyrics to the situation. 'A Momentary Lapse of Reason' comes from 'One Slip', a song that appears to be about one of those after the party quick affairs, wham bam on the coats on the bed and not even a thank you ma'am to distinguish it, but in a band like this there have been many such lapses, from Syd's sad decline from fauna into flora to Roger's 'One of these days I'm going to cut you up into little pieces' scream of rage.

The other alternative title comes from 'Sorrow', and it could be about me . . . or you . . . or Dave . . . or, yes, Roger:

> *There's an unceasing wind that blows through this night*
> *And there's dust in my eyes that blinds my sight*
> *And silence that speaks so much louder than words*
> *Of promises broken*

And to me the promise isn't a pledge, it's a potential, the might-have-been that still lingers around the Sixties dream.

Listen, let me own up. I think the new Floyd is brilliant, whatever they call it. It breaks very little new ground, that's true, and it plays as if punk and reggae and funk and the Afro-beat never happened, which to me is no bad thing. It's more varied, musically, than anything they've done since Umma-Gumma, and also more varied in terms of mood.

If you want black despair, you'll find it there in 'A New Machine' (a lyric which reminds me rather of one thing Roger once said to me about him: 'Dave's mask is very thick and efficient. I hate to think of the pain underneath it all, under the benign, everything's-cool-man exterior, which he doesn't allow himself contact with. I dunno, he may himself contact with it, he certainly doesn't allow anyone else any contact with it.' I wonder if Roger remembers it was Dave who wrote so powerfully about being 'Comfortably Numb', in 'The Wall').

And 'The Dogs of War', which could have been a rather facile commentary on the world of the SAS and Irangate (on the studio TV all day in LA, while Dave mixed and remixed and remixed the album), and certainly does not spare the political murderers. It also sees the roots of their actions in all of us:

> *We all have a dark side, to say the least*
> *Dealing in death is the nature of the beast*

172

Matter of fact, it's all dark, as you might say.

There is even a religious song (I can call it nothing more), using as a metaphor Dave's recent excursions into solo piloting, which contrasts humanity's angelic aspirations with our more mundane realities:

> *Can't keep my eyes from the circling sky*
> *Tongue-tied and twisted, just an earthbound misfit,*
> *I*
> '*Learning to Fly*'

Roger's album, in contrast, could only have been made in the late eighties. It is as contemporary as the image he created for the 1987 Adrian Boot colour photographs, silk suit, street-cool shades, confident camera gaze and all. Could this be the man so paranoid about possible attack that he refused to be photographed, ever, donning the featureless mask from 'The Wall' when Rolling Stone wanted to put him on the cover? This is a new Roger indeed.

Subject-wise, however, this is old Roger Waters' territory. We are back in the world of non-communication, first explored at the time of 'Meddle', in which the catatonic son of a Welsh coal miner communicates with the world (and eventually the computers of the SDI star wars fantasies of Ronald Reagan) by tuning his idiot genius brain into radio waves.

Probably the best song is the funk-ish 'Who Needs Information', with its echoes of Lou Reed's 'Walk on the Wild Side'. But how many who hear its chorus (Who needs information/When you're working underground) will realise the song is about a coal miner?

Just as the Falklands occupied centre stage in 'The Final Cut', and terrorism provided the adrenalin flow that discomfitted in 'The Pro's and Cons', here the social background is there, too: the coal miner father is imprisoned for killing a scab-ferrying cab driver (something similar happened in our real life year-long miners' strike in 1984, only here it seems more like a prank that went wrong than an example of off-the-pithead violence), and Benny the vegetable manages in the end to drain away the power that fuels the death-dealing computers of the doomsday scenario.

But the album's real weakness is that, deprived of the synopsis, the listener would be hard put to it to know what the hell was going on, even if the vocoded voice of Billy was easier to decipher. And, neither in synopsis nor lyrics, is any successful attempt made to tie together the strands of the story, from the miners' strike to the nuclear threat, though the black miners digging out Namibian uranian to fuel the

British deterrent could explain it to you in just a few, well-chosen words.

The album ends with a song inspired by Live Aid, 'The Tide is Turning', which has a nice line in hope:

> *I'm not saying that the battle is won*
> *But on Saturday night all those kids in the sun*
> *Wrested technology's sword from the hands of the War Lords . . .*

Is that what they did? What they really did? Then how come today, two years later, people are still picketing Greenham Common, painting the cruising missile wagons as they lumber about the countryside, the women being pulled out of their polythene shelters and getting their noses pressed into the mud by our ever-trusty British bobbies, and all in the cause of the special relationship which allows the CIA and MI5 to conspire against the legally elected Government of these tight little islands?

It is not to deny the significance of Band Aid and its many spin-offs to realise that it did not, not even for a moment, ever try to grab the sword out of the hands of its bearers. The significance of what Geldof did was individual, even symbolic, in that in the world of Thatcherite hard-nosed Victorian laissez-faire and Reaganomics, the voices of millions spoke up for caring, and the term 'do-gooder' lost its pejorative sense.

The use of the Pontardulais Male Voice Choir, a group from the Welsh mining valleys who also sang in 'The Wall' movie, links the song thematically with what's gone before in Roger's career, but in the end it has to be admitted, reluctantly, it's true, that the whole thing fails to jell.

Interestingly, the Floyd's album also ends with a song inspired by Live Aid. It deals with matters on a less cosmic level, looking into the hearts of all (and there is some of this in all of us) who turn away from the pictures of avoidable starvation on the News at Ten, who try to forget the lessons we should have learned at Dachau and Nuremberg, still news in the Klaus Barbie trial thirty years after the OSS smuggled him away from American-occupied Germany, still news in Soweto and Managua and Seoul and everywhere else the money men wield the bomb and the gun and the rubber truncheon to hold on to their crumbling power.

Though Dave is still upset by the time I once called him an old Tory, I'm sure he'd admit he's not the most political of animals, but 'On the Turning Away' strikes me as one of the great human anthems that come round once every few years, like 'Give Peace a Chance' and

174

'We Shall Overcome' and 'If I had a Hammer' and 'Down by the Riverside', which gives the struggle a human face:

> *No more turning away*
> *From the weak and the weary*
> *No more turning away*
> *From the coldness inside*
> *Just a world that we all must share*
> *It's not enough just to stand and stare*
> *Is it only a dream that there'll be*
> *No more turning away?*

Dave bridled when I asked if the tune's Celtic tinge was a tip of the hat to Geldof. 'I'm a Celt myself, don't forget,' he said (and aren't we all closet Celts under skin in these islands, as I once pointed out to Alan Stivell, whose pan-Celticism would have to appeal to all of us, or none?). 'I'm also an old folkie from way back.'

There is certainly, to be sure, a ring about it of the McPeakes' Will Ye Go, Lassie, Go, the song from the Nationalist stronghold of Fermanagh which Dylan tried with such manifest lack of success to turn into a sing-along all those years ago at his Isle of Wight Pop Festival come-back.

So where does all this leave us, 22 years after that first £15 Floyd gig at the Countdown Club, that Friday night in 1965? I could be sad, if the new album wasn't so inspiring, and I still am sad as one always is when old friends fall out. Yet 22 years is a long time for any job. Its longer than most marriages, for God's sake, and working in a band like the Floyd must be a lot like a marriage. And like most marriages, when they break up, it's kind of messy.

And while the legal eagles rub their hands, instead of alimony there is the enormous capital value of a name which still carries a lot of clout in the world of music business, if the way the Ottawa Floyd concerts sold out in a couple of days is any guide. Despite the millions the Norton Warburg crash cost them, it's still got to be worth even more millions.

As of this time of writing, it appears that Pink Floyd consists basically of Dave Gilmour and Nick Mason, with Richard Wright pulling down a salary for whatever contributions he may make, plus interesting guests like Joni Mitchell's old associate, Tom Scott, responsible for the fine sax on 'Terminal Frost' on side one of the album, and Scott Page, who will be repeating his rather more raunchy 'Dogs of War' sax solo on the marathon tour beginning in September 1987.

I say that's the way it appears, because clearly Roger Waters contests their right to use the title in which he has at least a fourth interest. He feels, and I sympathise with that view, that it's time for them to pursue their several destinies as solo artists. Certainly, he is putting his money where his mouth is, after having lost an admitted half-million with his Hitch-hiking tour, and will be back on the touring treadmill (which he has always hated) at much the same time Floyd will be re-conquering the world.

The problem is that none of them – and this includes Roger – appears to be capable of producing anything as musically powerful on their own as they have collectively. Bands like Floyd – and the Byrds and Fairport Convention are similar to them in this respect – appear to have a life of their own, much more than the sum of their individual parts, which is not dependent upon the presence of any one individual. Between 'Dark Side' and 'Final Cut', you could have been excused for thinking that Floyd was Roger's band, and right now it seems more like Dave's. In fact, it doesn't seem to belong to either of them, still less to any of the money men now snorting eagerly round the trough. It was the creation of a time, now gone, and hopes, still very much here and now, and in a sense it belongs to all of us.

When I heard they were 're-forming' (having never officially disbanded), I must confess I sighed a little petulant sigh of irritation in sympathy with Roger's wish to close the door on the era. When I was about to hear the two new albums, I *knew* that Roger's would be the most relevant to today, and expected Floyd, at best, to merely recycle the old effects as if Altamont and the Falklands had never happened.

Well, I was wrong. Floyd's new album is a new classic and Roger's is . . . well . . . Roger's.

Comparisons, as Shakespeare didn't quite say, are odious. I don't want to get into the tedius business of assessing Roger's album against the Floyd's, because the one thing they both prove is how far they have moved apart, and why he was obviously right to leave. Roger's album is his album, and it's where he is today, and I'm sure the contemporary feel to a lot of the rhythms is because that's what moves him. Similarly, though Dave's pot belly and fourteen o'clock shadow when he played me the mixes of the new album up in the Primrose Hill studio in the early hours mark him down as another of us ageing hippies, 'Of Promises Broken', 'A Momentary Lapse of Reason', call it what you will, is where we all are today too, like it or not, whatever walls we may build up between one way of looking at the world, and the other.

They're both sincere reactions to their specific situations, and if one speaks to me more clearly than the other, then you may have the opposite reaction, depending on where you were then (or if you were even born), and where you have got to since.

In the end, as the Psalmist says, all flesh is grass.

But before the bonfire comes, we blossom in our own way, and spread our own seeds.

Inshallah.

KARL DALLAS

APPENDIX

How to Lose £3.3 Million on Skateboards and Langoustines

From the Financial Times, June 30, 1987:

BUSINESSMAN JAILED FOR FRAUD ON SMALL INVESTORS

Mr Andrew Warburg, a City businessman, was jailed for three years yesterday for a multi-million-pound swindle that deprived hundreds of small investors of their life savings or retirement nest-eggs. When his company crashed in 1981, investors lost about £2.5 million, the Old Bailey was told.

Warburg, a 43-year-old chartered accountant, of Wallington, Surrey, admitted fraudulent trading and false accounting between October 1978 and March 1981. Mrs Barbara Mills QC for the prosecution said his company – Norton Warburg – persuaded the public to invest cash for his firm to manage on their behalf. Clients included retired Bank of England employees. 'By the time the company collapsed, 400 people had invested with them. These funds often either represented their life savings or sums they had acquired on their retirement.'

Warburg set up his company in 1973 when he was 29, but by October 1978 he was already insolvent. Until then the company had operated properly and honestly, according to Mr Vivian Robinson QC, who defended Warburg in court. The Bank of England's pension section even recommended Norton Warburg to its retiring employees.

One of its 'substantial' investors had been the pop group Pink Floyd, Mr Robinson noted. But in September 1978 the group ended its agreement and withdrew £860,000, putting the company in a 'very difficult position'.

This is a cautionary tale, though one with no moral, except, perhaps, 'you can't trust nobody no-how these days'. It was back in February 1973 that Andrew Oscar Warburg, then a rising star in the insurance brokers Scott Warburg and Partners, left the company to branch out on his own, taking tax specialist Melvin Perera and six other employees with him.

Pretty soon, he had attracted a glittering roster of show biz and sporting personalities, Kate Bush, Bee-Gee Barry Gibb, cricketer Colin Cowdrey and of course the Floyd, among them. The logic of such people putting their money to work with Warburg and his associates was immaculate: after all, the talent to write a good song or make a hit album doesn't mean you know how to read the fine print on a profit-and-loss account, and it made sense to go to the real professionals when it came to managing the £3–5 million a year they were reputed to be making out of song and record royalties – they received a £4½ million advance for 'The Wall'.

Before Floyd came along, Norton Warburg had about £200,000 to manage, but the company really began to grow once they had the Floyd four under contract and paying about £300,000 a year for services which are said to have included secretarial, financial and insurance broking.

They had the £860,000 mentioned in the FT report on deposit, and also invested large sums – said to total about £3.3 million – in venture capital projects.

Things started promisingly, with fairly modest profits being made on a security printing business, Rochford Thompson, a water purifying business, Fluid Dynamics, a company manufacturing carbon fibre boats, Carbocraft, and a property deal in London's Cadogan Gardens. Total profit: about £125,000.

Then the losses began to be reported. They bought a 55.6 per cent holding in the Moorhead Hotel in Devon for £150,000 and a 60 per cent stake in Moorhead Farm Products for £21,000 – but they only got £30,000 of their money back when they sold them. In all, Norton Warburg invested £2,636,000 of their money: 60 per cent of the Willows Canal floating restaurant for £180,000, 55 per cent of Celtic Foods for £150,000, 80 per cent of Celtic Seafare for £170,000, 55 per cent of the Benjyboards skateboard company for £215,000, £250,000 ploughed into Escalopes car traders, £1,500,000 in Cossack Securities, which was compulsorily wound-up by the Banque Brussels Lambert in January, 1981.

Willows Canal was insolvent in 1979, so were the two Celtic Companies and Benjyboards, though the previous year Norton Warburg were forecasting a £72,000 profit from 'a plentiful supply of langoustine being processed on the east coast at Dunbar and on the west coast at Campbeltown'. While they acknowledged in the same report that the bottom had dropped out of the skateboard market, creating 'low sales and high stock levels', 'a large quantity of slow-moving/dead stock is expected to be sold to Arab countries at good prices within a month'.

That was in September 1978. The following year Benjyboards went bust.

Floyd also put a lot of money into Norton Warburg Investments: nearly half a million, giving them a 20 per cent stake in the company. Some of this company's investments, like the 60 per cent it bought of the My Kinda Town Limited pizza chain, were successful, but many others weren't. In 1981, managing director Steven Gee was promising to pay investors back between 8p and 40p in the pound.

It's easy to see the Floyd four as being gullible – and possibly victims of their own greed. But a lot of other respectable city gents also got taken in.

As the FT report says, the Bank of England were recommending Norton Warburg to their own pensioners, and among the Floyd's fellow shareholders in Norton Warburg Investments were bluechip establishments like Legal and General, Gartmore Trust and Touche Remnant.

Not all their investments produced such poor results. Britannia Row, the facilities company responsible for all their special effects, lighting, and sound, continued to return on the £3 million they ploughed into it. When you are paying out a quarter of a million for equipping just one leg of a world tour (the estimated costs for the American 'Wall' concerts) it makes sense to have it done in-house.

Newspapers have valued Roger Waters' home at £2 million, and members of the group also own a couple of houses in the South of France, two houses in Rhodes, two in London, two manor houses in the country.

All this puts them in a rather different league from the widow with a deaf and dumb child who lost £10,000 she had set aside for her son's future in the Norton Warburg crash. Dave still runs his Porsche and Roger still has his French impressionists. It is hard to be very upset about their missing millions, when the coffers are still being topped up at a similar rate, especially now that one entire German factory is doing nothing but turn out compact disc copies of 'Dark Side of the Moon'.

Perhaps the real moral is this: You can't beat the system. Or not by trying to join it.

Afterword

Pink Floyd's U.S. tour was boosted by strong sales of the new album, lacking Waters' involvement, 'A Momentary Lapse of Reason,' which hit the number 14 spot on LP and number 2 on the CD list. The new touring ensemble included bassist Tony Levin, sax man Tom Scott, guitarist Michael Landau and drummer Carmine Appice. Dave Gilmour told the *Washington Post* that Pink Floyd was fighting the effects of Water's last effort 'Final Cut' which "did real damage to the band."

Touring the States at the same time, Water's 'Radio K.A.O.S.' tour was favorably contrasted with the Pink Floyd tour by *The Chicago Tribune* which found the Floyd set "drab and turgid" whereas Waters "may not be able to write a melody to save his life" and had a presence and message "often bilious and misanthropic" — but then again, they concluded, at least he had both presence and a message. General response however was different: one teenager quoted at a Floyd concert said: It's the same music, whoever's putting it out." The Pink Floyd name was what people turned out for and Waters' tour suffered accordingly.

Interviewed the following January by the *Chicago Tribune*, Nick Mason attested plausibly that, despite public rancor between Gilmour and Waters, he himself found the whole thing "very sad and very disappointing" and would have "loved to sneak in and see his show.... In fact the only reason we didn't all go when we were in Toronto at the same time was that all the arguments had begun to surface in the press and it would have turned into a zoo."

In June 1988, Pink Floyd followed up his U.S. tour with two consecutive dates at France's music festival, playing to crowds of more than 160,000 at the Palace as Versailles. In November, Gilmour and Mason accompanied French President Francois Mitterand to the Soviet Space Center at Baikonur to watch the launch of a French-Soviet manned space craft. Soviet News Agency TASS reported Gilmour and Mason as saying "they would sound out the possibility of flying in a Soviet aircraft" and further speculated that watching the launch would "inspire Nick and David to write another cycle of their 'space' music." A cassette of 'Dark Side of the Moon' was given to the cosmonauts, to be played near the title site.

In June 1989, Pink Floyd was back in the Soviet Union, playing the largest ever show in the Eastern bloc by a Western pop-group. Soviet authorities defrayed the band's costs by providing cargo crafts for over a hundred tons of equipment since, as Gilmour put it, "the costs are enormous so we [were] probably paying for the privilege of playing here."

In July, despite local political protest and controversy, Pink Floyd played on a floating stage, thirty feet from the bank of famous landmark St. Mark's Palace in Venice. Fifty thousand people poured into the site where no toilet facilities, nor supervision of trash-disposal had been provided.

The mess of rubbish and human waste which

182

accumulated, sometimes literally in the doors of historic churches, resulted in the resignation of six Socialist Councillors from the Venice City council. Two councilors were subsequently charged and tried for costing the public purse an estimated $47,000 in damage to public property because of their decision to let Pink Floyd play and for making no provisions for the concert. Safety precautions before the concert had been limited to the insistence by one councilor that Pink Floyd cut down their wattage from one hundred plus kilowatts to a mere sixty.

Later that month a concert at the site of the torn down Berlin Wall saw Roger Waters reunited with Pink Floyd for a charity performance of 'The Wall' before an audience of 150,000 and a global TV audience which included, incidentally, war-torn Beirut. A temporary cease-fire allowed entertainment-needy Beirutis to catch a gig, transmitted via Saudi Arabia. Waters additionally agreed to donate all publishing royalties from a live album of the show to charity.

In August 1990, Nick Mason had a feature interview in *Autoweek*, discussing his extensive collection of racing cars. The interview included such controversial musical statements as "Some Ferraris should be red, but you need other colors as well." In October 1991, a few of the band's members were injured when their car overshot an embankment at a race near San Luis Potosi, Mexico. Steve O'Rourke broke a leg and Dave Gilmour suffered facial cuts and bruises to the head, but Mason was "only slightly injured" and continued the race in his Jaguar.

That same month, 'Dark Side of the Moon' topped

the list of albums being certified multi-platinum at the Recording Industry Association of America's gold and platinum certifications. The album had sold twelve million units, eighteen years after its release.

In February 1992, the *Daily Mail of London* announced that Waters and his wife of seventeen years, Carolyne, were separating. He, it was purported, had "another love" in L.A. where he was recording a new album; she was "devastated" and said "there's no-one else in my life." The "someone else" was Pricilla Phillips, an actress and aristocratic bon vivant friend of Duchess of Kent Sarah Ferguson. Pricilla and Waters were still "about to marry" in July 1993 when Nigel Dempster reviewed their relationship in his *Daily Mail* gossip column.

In May 1992, Sony released the 65 minute music video of racing-car footage, shot during the race that resulted in the injuries, and 18 minutes of new Pink Floyd instrumentals written for the film.

October 1992 saw Waters release a new album 'Amused to Death' which included such apolitical lyrics as:

> *God wants peace/God wants war*
> *God wants famine/God wants chain stores*

Waters characterized the album as being "about the relationship between human beings and television" and the drift of foreign policy toward being "entertainment for the folk back home." It sold moderately well.

The Pink Floyd boxed set released in December 1992 had no cuts at all off the last Waters' album 'Final Cut,' and also none of their film soundtrack work. Waters' objections, related to 'The Wall,' were over-ruled since all votes came down to his one against the other three.

Gilmour claimed in interviews that the estimated initial project came to seventeen CD's and was complete, but the company felt the public purse would not bear it. The resulting set had ten discs and no out-takes or un-released tracks. Gilmour asserted that the band didn't make any out-takes. Gilmour also told *The Chicago Tribune* that one reason he refused to give up the Pink Floyd name was that he'd spent "every year since [he'd] been 21 ... building this brand name, if you like .. I've earned it and I'm unwilling to let it go."

Waters' objections were that tracks from 'The Wall,' an album in part about greed and especially stadium-concert greed, would go on the box set and, in general would be played by the other Floyd members in stadiums. In interviews, Gilmour tends to downplay Waters' leadership and hype the over-all unit Pink Floyd.

In a moment of candor with *The Boston Globe*, Gilmour admitted a loss:

"Roger was the king of the lyrics, and we kind of miss that. But we're concentrating at trying to do things the way we used to do them - jamming around.." Asked if there is a burden bearing the legacy of Pink Floyd, he replied, "of course there is, but it's not something that can't be borne, that can't be lifted and carried. I do my best."

Pink Floyd have announced they will embark on their first world tour in five years in March 1994.

INDEX

188

189

191

192